THE OFFICIAL Pokémon™ Handbook

THE OFFICIAL

Pokémon

Handbook

by Maria S. Barbo

SCHOLASTIC INC.
New York Toronto London Auckland Sydney
Mexico City New Delhi Hong Kong

For my brother, who introduced me to video games

ISBN 0-439-10397-5

12 11 10 9 8 7 6   9/9 0 1 2 3 4/0

Printed in the U.S.A.
First Scholastic printing, July 1999

A WORD FROM PROFESSOR OAK

Welcome to the Pokémon legend! I'm Professor Oak. I guess you could call me something of an expert on all things Pokémon. (That's pronounced POH-kay-mahn.) Over the years I've seen hundreds of new trainers get their very first Pokémon — including my own grandson, Gary. I don't collect my own Pokémon anymore. (I like to leave all the running around to the young folk.) But I do teach the basics to the new generation of Pokémon trainers.

Your mission: To collect and train as many of the 150 known species of Pokémon as you can. I supply many trainers with their first Pokémon. Usually I let them choose between three beginning Pokémon — Bulbasaur, Charmander, and Squirtle. Once you have your first Pokémon, you can battle and catch other Pokémon.

Your **allies and friends** are Ash, Misty, and Brock — fellow Pokémon trainers and breeders.

Your **enemies?** The evil Team Rocket: Jessie, James, their sinister Pokémon, Meowth, and their boss, Giovanni. They're determined to fight what they call the "evils" of truth and love, while they capture and control all rare Pokémon. (Ooh — I just can't stand to think about the way they mistreat all those poor, innocent Pokémon!) If they're not stopped, they may take over the world!

Your **biggest rival** is my grandson, Gary. You'll probably battle him a couple of times along the way. He's determined to be the best, that grandson of mine — and he's well on his way, too!

Your **goal** may be to become the **world's greatest**

Pokémon master, like Ash — to win every battle, collect all 150 Pokémon, and join the ranks of the master trainers in the Pokémon League.

Or you may

prefer to be a **great Pokémon breeder,** like Brock, and learn how to raise the best Pokémon and to bring out their inner strength and

personality. Or you may just want to **collect** and train Pokémon of a particular element, like Misty. Her specialty is Water element Pokémon.

Not into the battle aspect? No need to be. Pokémon make loving and faithful friends and companions.

Whatever you decide, you'll have to know as much as you can about your Pokémon. Pokémon won't listen to just anyone. They are looking for friends, not masters. The more you know about your Pokémon, the more techniques you will be able to teach them, and the closer you and your Pokémon will become.

That's why I have prepared this Pokédex for each Pokémon trainer. It's full of information and advice about Pokémon and their training. You'll want to keep it handy as you're watching the cartoon, playing the game, trading with a friend, or deciding which Pokémon to add to your growing collection. Use it as your guide. Read it carefully. Ask it questions. It's got everything you need to know inside.

Well, now you must be eager to get on your way. There are a lot of Pokémon to catch — and many, many things to learn.

Good luck!

Professor Oak

THE POKÉMON JOURNEY

Pokémon are creatures that come in all shapes, sizes, and personalities. Some live in oceans, others in caves, old towers, rivers, or tall grass. Some Pokémon are plantlike; some are animallike. And some are even ghostlike!

There are **150 different species** of Pokémon. Within each species are tons of individual Pokémon. Some Pokémon are very common, like Pidgey and Rattata. You can find them almost anywhere. Other Pokémon, like Articuno, are so rare there's only one of them in the whole world.

Each **individual Pokémon** has its own personality. For example, there are a

lot of Pikachu, but Ash has a very special one that travels with him on his adventures.

Becoming a Pokémon trainer is a fun, exciting, sometimes dangerous, and always interesting experience. Pokémon live untamed and untrained in the wild. When you turn ten years old, you are eligible to receive a license from the Pokémon League to begin your quest as a Pokémon trainer. As Professor Oak said, your mission is to go on a **Pokémon journey** collecting individuals

from each of the 150 species of Pokémon. Then you can teach them how to grow into the best Pokémon they can be. You will train them for battle, trade them with other trainers, and most importantly, become their friend.

Your journey takes place in cities, forests, rivers, oceans, caves, and the roads in between. The **towns and cities** are the centers of action. Each one has a Pokémon Center where Pokémon can recover after each battle. You can also log on to the computers there to check in with Professor Oak in order to see how you're doing compared to other trainers, and store your Pokémon in a special storage system.

There are also Poké Marts that sell Poké Balls and other

supplies, and a gym where you can practice battling with other trainers and test your skills against the gym leader.

Trainers start their quest in their own hometown. Ash Ketchum and many other new trainers begin their journey in **Pallet Town**. That's where Professor Oak — *the* Pokémon expert — has his lab. He gives all of Pallet Town's new trainers their very first Pokémon and their own Pokédex. But the outskirts of town are definitely *not* boring. The towns and cities are connected by paths, grassy fields, and forests. This is where most of the wild Pokémon live. That means tons of Pokémon to battle, catch, and add to your growing collection.

Keep in mind that each Pokémon is special. They won't stand to be mistreated. If you put a Pokémon into a situation that it doesn't like, or if you're mean to it, it won't listen to you. It might even go to sleep in the middle of a battle. Most of all, Pokémon just want to be your Poké friends!

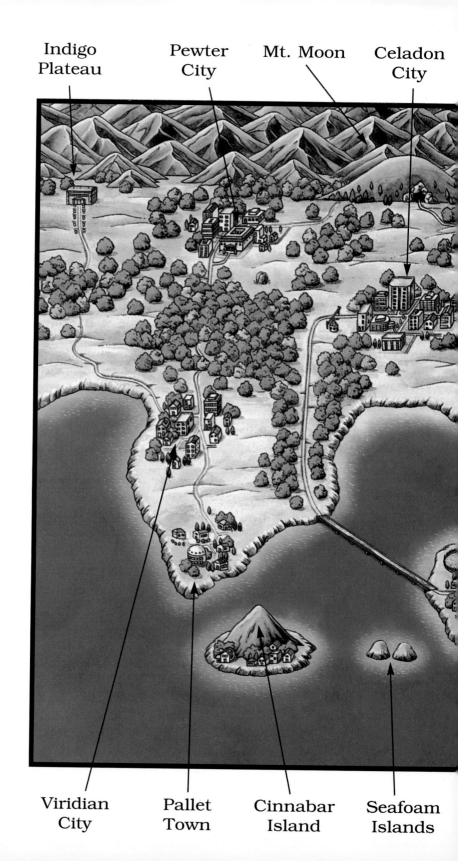

Indigo
Plateau

Pewter
City

Mt. Moon

Celadon
City

Viridian
City

Pallet
Town

Cinnabar
Island

Seafoam
Islands

Cerulean
City

Sea
Cottage

Saffron
City

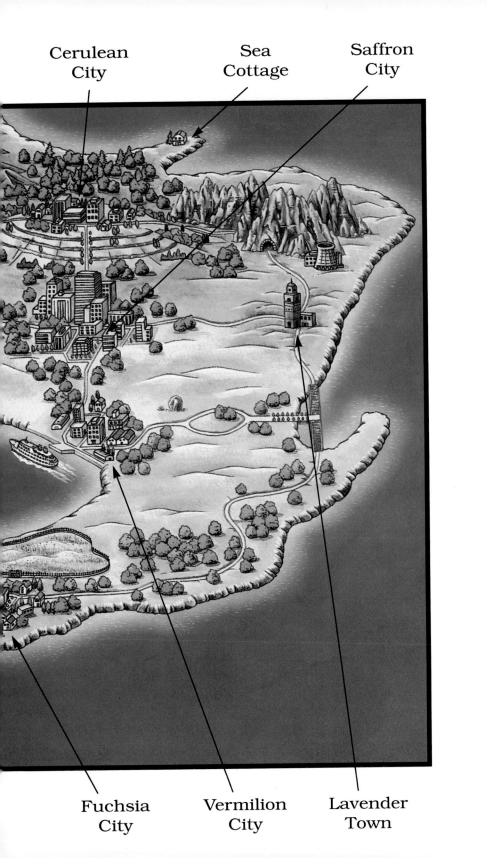

Fuchsia
City

Vermilion
City

Lavender
Town

BATTLE BASICS

Why battle? There are two basic reasons for a Pokémon to battle. One is for sport. You can battle another trainer in a friendly competition. Your Pokémon do the fighting, but you decide which Pokémon and which techniques, or  attacks, to use. Battles for sport are important because your Pokémon gains valuable experience, learns new techniques, sharpens old techniques, and evolves to the next level much more quickly. Plus — it's fun! Pokémon like to play.

The second good reason to battle is to capture wild Pokémon. Wild Pokémon have no training and no owners. They can usually be found in long grass, dungeons, or water (you'll need fishing rods to catch these) — and sometimes in amusement parks like the Safari Zone and the Coin Exchange. Battle is one of the main ways to collect a Pokémon. You can also buy them in some stores or trade for them with friends. Other trainers' Pokémon are off-limits, however. You can't capture their Pokémon even if you win a competition.

Choose the best Pokémon for the job. Each trainer can carry around a team of up to six Pokémon at a time. For  each new situation you encounter, you will decide which six Pokémon it is most advantageous to carry with you. The rest are kept in a high-tech computer storage system. You can use as many of the six Pokémon you are carrying in a single battle as you want. Feel free to switch at any  time — especially if the Pokémon who's fighting looks like it's taking a beating. If you win a battle, each Pokémon that fought gains experience.

The longer you train, the more you'll learn about keeping a team with a variety of techniques and strengths. You'll also learn which Pokémon are best suited to which battles.

The Face-off. In the gym or on the road, other trainers are eager to show off their Pokémon techniques. If another trainer challenges you to a friendly competition, you must accept. It's rude to refuse.

Don't think you'll get off easy, either. Your team will have to face and hopefully defeat each and every Pokémon on the other trainer's team. You win when your Pokémon have defeated all of the other trainer's

Pokémon. A Pokémon is defeated when it gets so weak that it faints.

So what's in it for you? In addition to all the experience your Poké friends gain, you earn a cash prize for every competition you win. It's money you'll need to buy valuable supplies.

The Poké Ball. To capture a Pokémon, you'll need a Poké Ball. Poké Balls are what you carry your Pokémon around in while they are learning and training. Only one creature fits in each ball, so you'll have to keep a good supply on hand. Most Pokémon will only leave their Poké Balls when you command them to. Some may complain about being in a Poké

Ball, but only Pikachu will refuse to get in.

The Capture. Pokémon never die in battle. They just get very weak and may even faint! The goal in any battle with a wild Pokémon is to get its down energy low enough to capture it — but not down so low that it faints. If it does, that Pokémon goes straight back to the wild.

Once the wild Pokémon is weak, it's Poké Ball time. Throw a ball at it. And remember, there are no guarantees. A weakened Pokémon may still break out of the ball. If it doesn't, it's yours to train and will — hopefully — be loyal only to you.

NOTE: Health and energy do not automatically return to the Pokémon just because you capture it. You'll have to take care of your Poké friend before it can fight for you.

HOW TO USE THIS BOOK

Number: Each Pokémon has one. If you're not sure of a Pokémon's number, there is an alphabetical checklist in the back of this book.

Pronunciation: How to say the Pokémon's name.

Type: Within each element of Pokémon, there are types. For example, a Water element Pokémon could be fishlike, turtlelike, or ducklike! What kind of Water Pokémon is it? Check out each Pokémon's type for more detailed info.

Height and **Weight:** The Pokémon in these pictures may all look the same size — but don't be fooled! Pokémon come in a bunch of different shapes and sizes. Some are tiny, and some are *huge*!

Techniques: Each Pokémon starts off with a set of battle attacks — such as Scratch or Tackle. These are the strategies, or attacks, a Pokémon uses to win a battle. It is how they fight.

Other Techniques: As a Pokémon gains more experience, it can learn new, more powerful techniques. These tend to be determined by their element — like Flamethrower for a Fire element. **NOTE:** A Pokémon can only remember four techniques at a time. As it learns new techniques, it may forget the old ones.

Good Against: Your Pokémon has a good chance of winning against these elements in battle — even if the two have the same amount of experience. For example, Fire elements will usually melt Ice elements.

Bad Against: Your Pokémon is at a definite disadvantage in battle against these elements. Think about choosing another member of your team for battles against these Pokémon.

Evolves at Level: Each Pokémon starts at level one. The more experience the Pokémon gains, the higher its level becomes. If your Pokémon has a normal evolution style, it will only evolve when it reaches a certain level. That level is different for each Pokémon. Look here to see what level your Pokémon has to reach before it will evolve.

PRONUNCIATION:
BUL-BUH-SORE

ELEMENT:
GRASS/POISON

TYPE:
SEED

HEIGHT:
2' 4"

WEIGHT:
15 LBS

TECHNIQUES:
TACKLE, GROWL

OTHER TECHNIQUES:
LEECH SEED,
VINE WHIP,
POISON POWDER,
RAZOR LEAF,
GROWTH,
SLEEP POWDER,
SOLAR BEAM

GOOD AGAINST:
WATER

BAD AGAINST:
FIRE, POISON,
FLYING, DRAGON,
GHOST

EVOLUTION:
NORMAL

EVOLVES AT LEVEL:
16

In this book, each element has a color. For example, Fire is red, Poison is purple, and Ground is brown. Look here to help you figure out which color represents which element. If a Pokémon has two colors, it is two elements.

Element: Tells you what kind of characteristics and techniques your Pokémon will have. For example, Water elements usually live in rivers, lakes, or oceans and have techniques like Bubble and Hydro Pump. Elements also clue you in to which Pokémon would do well in a battle against another element. Water dampens Fire, and Fire scorches Grass. It's kind of like a more advanced version of rock, paper, scissors.

Personality quirks, secrets, training tips — basically, everything else you need to know about this Pokémon.

Bulbasaur is a strong, manageable Pokémon for beginning trainers. No one's sure whether Bulbasaur and its evolutions are plant or animal. They seem to have the characteristics of both. A strange bulb was planted on Bulbasaur's back at birth. As Bulbasaur grows, the bulb becomes a large, leafy plant. Bulbasaur is in better shape than other beginning Pokémon like Charmander and Squirtle — which makes it harder to defeat and capture.

Evolution: Just like people, Pokémon don't stay the same forever. As they learn and grow they change form — they evolve! There are three basic ways a Pokémon can change into a higher form. **Normal** means they evolve or have evolved by gaining experience, learning new techniques, and moving to higher levels. **Special stones** — like Moon Stone or Thunder Stone — means the Pokémon can't evolve without this stone. Once you have the stone, you can use it to evolve your Pokémon whenever you want. **Trade** means that these Pokémon only move to the next stage after they've been traded to or from another game. They might evolve at a different speed or with different techniques than other Pokémon. **None** means these Pokémon don't evolve at all.

Pokédex Pick:
At a certain time of year Bulbasaur from all over the world gather together for a festival where they evolve.

Pokédex Pick: Fun facts to make you a true Pokémon master.

A quick and easy way to see all the stages of evolution the Pokémon will go through — what it was, is, and will be.

#01 BULBASAUR

PRONUNCIATION:
BUL-BUH-SORE

ELEMENT:
GRASS/POISON

TYPE:
SEED

HEIGHT:
2' 4"

WEIGHT:
15 LBS

TECHNIQUES:
TACKLE, GROWL

OTHER TECHNIQUES:
LEECH SEED,
VINE WHIP,
POISON POWDER,
RAZOR LEAF,
GROWTH,
SLEEP POWDER,
SOLAR BEAM

GOOD AGAINST:
WATER

BAD AGAINST:
FIRE, POISON,
FLYING, DRAGON,
GHOST

EVOLUTION:
NORMAL

EVOLVES AT LEVEL:
16

Bulbasaur is a strong, manageable Pokémon for beginning trainers. No one's sure whether Bulbasaur and its evolutions are plant or animal. They seem to have the characteristics of both. A strange bulb was planted on Bulbasaur's back at birth. As Bulbasaur grows, the bulb becomes a large, leafy plant. Bulbasaur is in better shape than other beginning Pokémon like Charmander and Squirtle — which makes it harder to defeat and capture.

Pokédex Pick:
At a certain time of year Bulbasaur from all over the world gather together for a festival where they evolve.

#02 IVYSAUR

PRONUNCIATION:
EYE-VEE-SORE

ELEMENT:
GRASS/POISON

TYPE:
SEED

HEIGHT:
3' 3"

WEIGHT:
29 LBS

TECHNIQUES:
TACKLE, GROWL, LEECH SEED, VINE WHIP

OTHER TECHNIQUES:
POISON POWDER, RAZOR LEAF, GROWTH, SLEEP POWDER, SOLAR BEAM

GOOD AGAINST:
WATER

BAD AGAINST:
FIRE, POISON, FLYING, DRAGON, GHOST

EVOLUTION:
NORMAL

EVOLVES AT LEVEL:
32

Pokémon that have two elements, like Ivysaur and Venusaur (they're Grass and Poison elements) have twice as many strengths and weaknesses as other Pokémon. As the bulb on Ivysaur's back grows, it gets harder for Ivysaur to stand on its hind legs.

#03 VENUSAUR

PRONUNCIATION:
VEE-NUH-SORE

ELEMENT:
GRASS/POISON

ELEMENT:
SEED

HEIGHT:
6' 7"

WEIGHT:
221 LBS

TECHNIQUES:
TACKLE, GROWL, LEECH SEED, VINE WHIP POISON POWDER, RAZOR LEAF

OTHER TECHNIQUES:
GROWTH, SLEEP POWDER, SOLAR BEAM

GOOD AGAINST:
WATER

BAD AGAINST:
FIRE, POISON, FLYING, DRAGON, GHOST

EVOLUTION:
NORMAL

When the bulb has bloomed into a full-sized flower like the one on Venusaur's back, the flower will absorb energy from the sun. Because of this, Venusaur has to keep moving to find more sunlight. The Leech Seed technique shared by both Ivysaur and Venusaur takes away an enemy's energy during battle.

#04 CHARMANDER

PRONUNCIATION:
CHAR-MAN-DER

ELEMENT:
FIRE

TYPE:
LIZARD

HEIGHT:
2' 0"

WEIGHT:
19 LBS

TECHNIQUES:
SCRATCH, GROWL

OTHER TECHNIQUES:
EMBER, LEER,
RAGE, SLASH,
FLAMETHROWER,
FIRE SPIN

GOOD AGAINST:
GRASS, ICE, BUG

BAD AGAINST:
FIRE, WATER,
ROCK, DRAGON

EVOLUTION:
NORMAL

EVOLVES AT LEVEL:
16

The cute, lizardlike Charmander is one of the Pokémon that Professor Oak often offers to new trainers. It has more attack power than Bulbasaur or Squirtle. And once it has lots of experience, it becomes almost impossible to beat — even against Water Pokémon.

Charmander has a flame on the tip of its tail and is hard to train even for skilled trainers. When it rains, steam spurts from Charmander's tail. If the flame ever goes out completely, Charmander might never be able to battle again.

PRONUNCIATION:
CHAR-MEAL-EE-EHN
ELEMENT:
FIRE
TYPE:
LIZARD
HEIGHT:
3' 7"
WEIGHT:
42 LBS
TECHNIQUES:
SCRATCH, GROWL, EMBER
OTHER TECHNIQUES:
LEER, RAGE, SLASH, FLAMETHROWER, FIRE SPIN
GOOD AGAINST:
GRASS, ICE, BUG
BAD AGAINST:
FIRE, WATER, ROCK, DRAGON
EVOLUTION:
NORMAL
EVOLVES AT LEVEL:
36

When Charmeleon swings its burning tail, the air around it gets hot, hot, hot. With its special Fire Spin technique, Charmeleon can attack two to five times in a row before its enemy can respond.

Pokédex Pick:

DAY CARE: School, homework, friends, chores… raising a team of Pokémon! Too much to handle? For a small fee, an expert babysitter in Cerulean City will help raise a Pokémon for you.

PRONUNCIATION:
CHAR-I-ZARD

ELEMENT:
FIRE/FLYING

TYPE:
LIZARD

HEIGHT:
5' 7"

WEIGHT:
200 LBS

TECHNIQUES:
SCRATCH, GROWL,
EMBER, LEER

OTHER TECHNIQUES:
RAGE, SLASH,
FLAMETHROWER,
FIRE SPIN

GOOD AGAINST:
GRASS, ICE,
FIGHTING, BUG

BAD AGAINST:
FIRE, WATER,
ROCK, DRAGON

EVOLUTION:
NORMAL

The fully evolved Charizard is on fire! The flames it spits are so hot, they can melt boulders. If Charizard gets carried away, it can start a forest fire.

Pokédex Pick:
Fire Pokémon like Charmeleon and Charizard are strong against Ice Pokémon, but not against Water Pokémon.

PRONUNCIATION:
SKWUR-TULL

ELEMENT:
WATER

TYPE:
TINY TURTLE

HEIGHT:
1' 8"

WEIGHT:
20 LBS

TECHNIQUES:
**TACKLE,
TAIL WHIP**

OTHER TECHNIQUES:
**BUBBLE, WATER GUN,
BITE, WITHDRAW,
SKULL BASH,
HYDRO PUMP**

GOOD AGAINST:
FIRE, GROUND, ROCK

BAD AGAINST:
**WATER, ELECTRIC,
GRASS, DRAGON**

EVOLUTION:
NORMAL

EVOLVES AT LEVEL:
16

This cute and cuddly turtlelike Pokémon is another one of the options Professor Oak has saved for you in his lab. It's a good first Pokémon. Some find Squirtle a little tougher to master than Bulbasaur or Charmander, but its amazing water techniques are definitely worth the effort.

In battle, Squirtle can use the Water Gun technique to spray a forceful foam from its mouth. Or it can use the Bubble technique to slow down an enemy. Squirtle makes a good friend for Pikachu.

PRONUNCIATION:
WAR-TOR-TULL

ELEMENT:
WATER

TYPE:
TURTLE

HEIGHT:
3' 3"

WEIGHT:
50 LBS

TECHNIQUES:
TACKLE, TAIL WHIP,
BUBBLE

OTHER TECHNIQUES:
WATER GUN, BITE,
WITHDRAW,
SKULL BASH,
HYDRO PUMP

GOOD AGAINST:
FIRE, GROUND, ROCK

BAD AGAINST:
WATER, ELECTRIC,
GRASS, DRAGON

EVOLUTION:
NORMAL

EVOLVES AT LEVEL:
36

As an older, more experienced turtle, Wartortle is more accomplished in the water than Squirtle. In fact, it likes to hide in the water when hunting prey — as a sneak attack. Wartortle has huge ears, like the rudders of a ship, which help it to balance when swimming fast.

PRONUNCIATION:
BLAST-OYS

ELEMENT:
WATER

TYPE:
SHELLFISH

HEIGHT:
5' 3"

WEIGHT:
189 LBS

TECHNIQUES:
TACKLE, TAIL WHIP, BUBBLE, WATER GUN

OTHER TECHNIQUES:
BITE, WITHDRAW, SKULL BASH, HYDRO PUMP

GOOD AGAINST:
FIRE, GROUND, ROCK

BAD AGAINST:
WATER, ELECTRIC, GRASS, DRAGON

EVOLUTION:
NORMAL

Blastoise has a big, hard shell that hides two very powerful, high-pressure water cannons. That means it can pump out hundreds of gallons of water (as much as is in an Olympic-sized pool) every minute! Blastoise uses its cannons for super-fast tackles.

Pokédex Pick:
NICKNAMES: Have more than one Squirtle? When you get a new Pokémon, you can give it a nickname. You can also change a Pokémon's nickname at the home of the Name Rater in Lavender Town.

#10 CATERPIE

This sweet little Pokémon is a lot like a caterpillar. It has short feet with suction cups on the ends that allow it to climb walls and trees without getting tired. Its String Shot slows down Caterpie's enemies. It doesn't take Capterpie long to evolve. You may want to stop its evolution and build up its experience for a while. Once Caterpie changes into a Metapod, it will not be able to move.

PRONUNCIATION:
CAT-ER-PEE

ELEMENT:
BUG

TYPE:
WORM

HEIGHT:
1' 0"

WEIGHT:
6 LBS

TECHNIQUES:
TACKLE, STRING SHOT

OTHER TECHNIQUES:
NONE

GOOD AGAINST:
GRASS, PSYCHIC

BAD AGAINST:
GHOST, FLYING, FIGHTING, FIRE

EVOLUTION:
NORMAL

EVOLVES AT LEVEL:
7

Pokédex Pick:
The first wild Pokémon Ash Ketchum ever caught was a Caterpie. Misty was terrified of it, just because it's a bug.

#11 METAPOD

PRONUNCIATION:
MET-UH-POD

ELEMENT:
BUG

TYPE:
COCOON

HEIGHT:
2' 4"

WEIGHT:
22 LBS

TECHNIQUES:
HARDEN

OTHER TECHNIQUES:
NONE

GOOD AGAINST:
GRASS, PSYCHIC

BAD AGAINST:
GHOST, FLYING, FIGHTING, FIRE

EVOLUTION:
NORMAL

EVOLVES AT LEVEL:
10

Metapod won't be in this form for a long time. But Caterpie needs to spend time as a Metapod before it can turn into a beautiful Butterfree. Just like a caterpillar in a cocoon, it can't move. Be sure to protect its weak and tender body from bird enemies like Pidgey and Spearow. Be patient with Metapod. A Butterfree is worth the wait!

PRONUNCIATION:
BUT-ER-FREE
ELEMENT:
BUG/FLYING
TYPE:
BUTTERFLY
HEIGHT:
3' 7"
WEIGHT:
71 LBS
TECHNIQUES:
NONE
OTHER TECHNIQUES:
CONFUSION,
POISON POWDER,
STUN SPORE,
SLEEP
POWDER,
SUPERSONIC,
WHIRLWIND,
PSYBEAM
GOOD AGAINST:
GRASS, BUGS,
PSYCHIC,
FIGHTING
BAD AGAINST:
GHOST, FLYING,
ELECTRIC, ROCK,
FIRE, FIGHTING
EVOLUTION:
NORMAL

Butterfree can fly! When fighting, Butterfree flaps its wings very fast, filling the air with toxic dust. Two of its favorite attacks are Sleep Powder, which sends an enemy snoozing, and Stun Spore, which paralyzes an enemy so it can't move. Be sure to keep lots of Awakening potion in your first-aid kit before doing battle with this beautiful but dangerous Pokémon.

Pokédex Pick:

Regretting that trade you made? Trade it back. Most trainers understand the bond that develops between a person and her/his Pokémon. When Ash traded his Butterfree — the very first Pokémon he had evolved on his own — for a Raticate, he realized they had been through too much together to be apart. So he traded back for it.

#13 WEEDLE

PRONUNCIATION:
WEE-DULL

ELEMENT:
BUG/POISON

TYPE:
HAIRY BUG

HEIGHT:
1' 0"

WEIGHT:
7 LBS

TECHNIQUES:
POISON STING,
STRING SHOT

OTHER
TECHNIQUES:
NONE

GOOD AGAINST:
GRASS,
FLYING,
PSYCHIC, BUG

BAD AGAINST:
GHOST,
FLYING,
FIGHTING,
FIRE, POISON,
GROUND,
ROCK

EVOLUTION:
NORMAL

EVOLVES AT LEVEL:
7

Weedle are usually found in forests, eating leaves. Weedle only have two techniques, but they are powerful. Like Caterpie, its String Shot slows down its enemies, and the sharp stinger on top of its head is poisonous. So be careful if you choose a Weedle as a pet.

#14 KAKUNA

PRONUNCIATION:
KA-KOO-NUH

ELEMENT:
BUG/POISON

TYPE:
COCOON

HEIGHT:
2' 0"

WEIGHT:
22 LBS

TECHNIQUES:
HARDEN

OTHER
TECHNIQUES:
NONE

GOOD AGAINST:
GRASS,
PSYCHIC, BUG

BAD AGAINST:
GHOST,
FLYING,
FIGHTING,
FIRE, POISON,
GROUND, ROCK

EVOLUTION:
NORMAL

EVOLVES AT LEVEL:
10

Like a Metapod, a Kakuna is a type of pod similar to the cocoon stage between a caterpillar and a butterfly. Kakuna can't move, so it can't attack. Its only defense is to harden its protective shell. You will have to be extra careful with Kakuna during this stage of evolution. But don't worry, Kakuna will be a Beedrill before you know it!

PRONUNCIATION:
BEE-DRILL

ELEMENT:
BUG/POISON

TYPE:
POISON BEE

HEIGHT:
3' 3"

WEIGHT:
65 LBS

TECHNIQUES:
NONE

OTHER TECHNIQUES:
FURY ATTACK,
FOCUS ENERGY,
TWINEEDLE, RAGE,
PIN MISSILE, AGILITY

GOOD AGAINST:
GRASS, PYCHIC, BUG

BAD AGAINST:
GHOST, FLYING,
FIGHTING, FIRE,
POISON, GROUND,
ROCK

EVOLUTION:
NORMAL

It has been a dangerous process, but now that this former Weedle has hatched, it is very strong. Beedrill are so fast, it's unbelievable. They attack using the large poisonous stingers on their front legs and tails. With practice, Beedrill will be able to learn techniques like Twineedle and Pin Missile increase the number of attacks they can launch in a row. Ouch! A Beedrill attack stings!

PRONUNCIATION:
PID-JEE

ELEMENT:
NORMAL/FLYING

TYPE:
TINY BIRD

HEIGHT:
I' 0"

WEIGHT:
4 LBS

TECHNIQUES:
GUST

OTHER TECHNIQUES:
**QUICK ATTACK,
SAND ATTACK,
WHIRLWIND,
WING ATTACK,
AGILITY,
MIRROR MOVE**

GOOD AGAINST:
**BUG, GRASS,
FIGHTING**

BAD AGAINST:
ROCK, ELECTRIC

EVOLUTION:
NORMAL

EVOLVES AT LEVEL:
18

Pidgey is very common in forests and woods. It is also the gentlest and easiest bird to capture. When on the ground, Pidgey flaps its wings extra hard to kick up sand and dust that blinds its opponents. Its Gust power creates tornadoes. Capturing a Pidgey is a good test of a beginning trainer's battle techniques.

#17 PIDGEOTTO

PRONUNCIATION:
PID-JYO-TOE

ELEMENT:
NORMAL/FLYING

TYPE:
BIRD

HEIGHT:
3' 7"

WEIGHT:
66 LBS

TECHNIQUES:
GUST,
SAND ATTACK,
QUICK ATTACK

OTHER
TECHNIQUES:
WHIRLWIND,
WING ATTACK,
AGILITY,
MIRROR MOVE

GOOD AGAINST:
BUG, GRASS,
FIGHTING

BAD AGAINST:
ROCK,
ELECTRIC

EVOLUTION:
NORMAL

EVOLVES AT LEVEL:
36

Unlike their mild-mannered cousin, Pidgeotto are very protective of their territory and will fiercely peck or claw at any intruder. Their Gust technique can blow away almost anyone or anything that gets in their way.

#18 PIDGEOT

PRONUNCIATION:
PID-JIT

ELEMENT:
NORMAL/FLYING

TYPE:
BIRD

HEIGHT:
4' 11"

WEIGHT:
87 LBS

TECHNIQUES:
GUST,
SAND ATTACK,
QUICK ATTACK,
WHIRLWIND,
WING ATTACK

OTHER
TECHNIQUES:
AGILITY,
MIRROR MOVE

GOOD AGAINST:
BUG, GRASS,
FIGHTING

BAD AGAINST:
ROCK,
ELECTRIC

EVOLUTION:
NORMAL

Pidgeotto's speed and sharpness increase as they evolve into Pidgeot. Pidgeot can fly 2 miles above the ground and faster than the speed of sound. When they hunt, Pidgeot fly on the surface of the water at top speed to catch unsuspecting Fish element prey like Magikarp.

#19 RATTATA

PRONUNCIATION:
RUH-TA-TAH

ELEMENT:
NORMAL

TYPE:
RAT

HEIGHT:
1' 0"

WEIGHT:
8 LBS

TECHNIQUES:
TACKLE,
TAIL WHIP

OTHER
TECHNIQUES:
QUICK ATTACK,
HYPER FANG,
FOCUS ENERGY,
SUPER FANG

GOOD AGAINST:
NONE

BAD AGAINST:
ROCK

EVOLUTION:
NORMAL

EVOLVES AT
LEVEL:
20

Rattata are very common. They have sharp teeth and will bite anything in an attack. They are small and very quick. Surprisingly, Rattata live peacefully with Pidgey.

Raticate use their whiskers to guide themselves and maintain balance. Without them, Raticate are very slow. The Hyper Fang technique that Rattata and Raticate share scares the enemy so much that it's afraid to attack back.

#20 RATICATE

PRONUNCIATION:
RAT-I-KATE

ELEMENT:
NORMAL

TYPE:
RAT

HEIGHT:
2' 4"

WEIGHT:
41 LBS

TECHNIQUES:
TACKLE,
TAIL WHIP,
QUICK ATTACK

OTHER
TECHNIQUES:
HYPER FANG,
FOCUS ENERGY,
SUPER FANG

GOOD AGAINST:
NONE

BAD AGAINST:
ROCK

EVOLUTION:
NORMAL

#21 SPEAROW

PRONUNCIATION:
SPEER-OH
ELEMENT:
NORMAL/FLYING
TYPE:
TINY BIRD
HEIGHT:
1' 0"
WEIGHT:
4 LBS
TECHNIQUES:
PECK, GROWL
OTHER TECHNIQUES:
LEER,
FURY ATTACK,
MIRROR MOVE,
DRILL PECK,
AGILITY
GOOD AGAINST:
BUG, GRASS,
FIGHTING
BAD AGAINST:
ROCK,
ELECTRIC
EVOLUTION:
NORMAL
EVOLVES AT LEVEL:
20

Don't let Spearow's size fool you. This little bird has a ferocious temper. Its Leer technique lowers an enemy's defenses. But Spearow has to flap its short wings very hard to stay in the air.

#22 FEAROW

PRONUNCIATION:
FEER-OH
ELEMENT:
NORMAL/FLYING
TYPE:
BEAK
HEIGHT:
3' 11"
WEIGHT:
84 LBS
TECHNIQUES:
PECK,
GROWL, LEER,
FURY ATTACK
OTHER TECHNIQUES:
MIRROR MOVE,
DRILL PECK,
AGILITY
GOOD AGAINST:
BUG, GRASS,
FIGHTING
BAD AGAINST:
ROCK,
ELECTRIC
EVOLUTION:
NORMAL

Unlike Spearow, Fearow has huge, regal wings. It can stay in the air for a long time without ever having to rest. At higher experience levels, it can use its Mirror Move to copy an enemy's attack.

#23 EKANS

PRONUNCIATION:
ECK-EHNS

ELEMENT:
POISON

TYPE:
SNAKE

HEIGHT:
6' 7"

WEIGHT:
15 LBS

TECHNIQUES:
WRAP, LEER

OTHER
TECHNIQUES:
POISON STING,
BITE, GLARE,
SCREECH, ACID

GOOD AGAINST:
GRASS, BUG

BAD AGAINST:
POISON,
GROUND, ROCK,
GHOST

EVOLUTION:
NORMAL

EVOLVES AT LEVEL:
22

Ekans is not a great Pokémon to keep around the house, especially if you have younger brothers and sisters. This cunning fighter is also one of Team Rocket's favorite Pokémon to use in battle.

Pokédex Pick:
Did you know that Ekans' name spelled backward is snake? Arbok's name spelled backward is Kobra.

#24 ARBOK

PRONUNCIATION:
AR-BOCK

ELEMENT:
POISON

TYPE:
COBRA

HEIGHT:
11' 6"

WEIGHT:
143 LBS

TECHNIQUES:
WRAP, LEER,
POISON STING

OTHER
TECHNIQUES:
BITE, GLARE,
SCREECH, ACID

GOOD AGAINST:
GRASS, BUG

BAD AGAINST:
POISON,
GROUND, ROCK,
GHOST

EVOLUTION:
NORMAL

Arbok is even worse. Rumor has it that the warning marks on Arbok's belly are different on different parts of its body. If successful, its Glare technique will paralyze an enemy. Arbok's Screech lowers an enemy's defenses.

Pokédex Pick:
Are sparks flying from your Pikachu's cheeks? That's an early sign of a cold in your electric rodent. It might be overcharged. Use up your Pikachu's extra energy in a playful battle, and it will be as good as new.

PRONUNCIATION:
PEEK-UH-CHEW

ELEMENT:
ELECTRIC

TYPE:
MOUSE

HEIGHT:
1' 4"

WEIGHT:
13 LBS

TECHNIQUES:
THUNDERSHOCK, GROWL

OTHER TECHNIQUES:
THUNDER WAVE, QUICK ATTACK, SWIFT, AGILITY, THUNDER

GOOD AGAINST:
WATER, FLYING

BAD AGAINST:
ELECTRIC, GRASS, DRAGON

EVOLUTION:
THUNDER STONE

Pika-pika-pika-chu! This super-cute lightning mouse is by far the most famous Pokémon of all. In fact, Team Rocket spends a lot of time trying to capture this rare Pokémon. Pikachu can zap an opponent with its electric power just by squeezing its cheeks. But be careful not to keep too many Pikachu in the same place. They have so much electricity, they can cause lightning storms and power outages in nearby cities!

Pikachu can be moody and shy, so it may take a while to get used to a new trainer. Be patient and treat Pikachu well, and you will soon be best buds. Remember, Pikachu *do not* like to be inside Poké Balls. It frightens them, so be gentle. If you get them angry, they will disobey you. Pikachu make good companions for Charmander and Squirtle.

PRONUNCIATION:
RYE-CHEW

ELEMENT:
ELECTRIC

TYPE:
MOUSE

HEIGHT:
2' 7"

WEIGHT:
66 LBS

TECHNIQUES:
THUNDERSHOCK,
GROWL,
THUNDER WAVE

OTHER TECHNIQUES:
NONE

GOOD AGAINST:
FLYING, WATER

BAD AGAINST:
ELECTRIC,
GRASS,
DRAGON

EVOLUTION:
NORMAL

Raichu has so much electrical power in its little body that it has to use its tail as a ground to avoid shocking itself! Its 10,000-volt Thunder Wave technique paralyzes an enemy so it can't move.

Pokédex Pick:
Sometimes Pikachu like their own personalities so much, they refuse to evolve into Raichu.

PRONUNCIATION:
SAND-SHROO

ELEMENT:
GROUND

TYPE:
MOUSE

HEIGHT:
2' 0"

WEIGHT:
26 LBS

TECHNIQUES:
SCRATCH

OTHER TECHNIQUES:
SLASH, POISON STING, SWIFT, FURY SWIPES, SAND ATTACK

GOOD AGAINST:
ELECTRIC, FIRE, POISON, ROCK

BAD AGAINST:
GRASS, BUG

EVOLUTION:
NORMAL

EVOLVES AT LEVEL:
22

Sandshrew burrow deep underground in hot, dry places. When Sandshrew uses Sand Attack, enemies have a hard time fighting back. Sandshrew make great pets if you live near a desert, but they are also tough to train because most of them are picky eaters.

#28 SANDSLASH

PRONUNCIATION:
SAND-SLASH

ELEMENT:
GROUND

TYPE:
MOUSE

HEIGHT:
3' 3"

WEIGHT:
65 LBS

TECHNIQUES:
SCRATCH,
SAND ATTACK,
SLASH

OTHER TECHNIQUES:
POISON STING,
SWIFT,
FURY SWIPES

GOOD AGAINST:
ELECTRIC, FIRE,
POISON, ROCK

BAD AGAINST:
GRASS, BUG

EVOLUTION:
NORMAL

When threatened, Sandslash curls up into a ball just like a porcupine. The spines on its back protect it from predators. Then it can roll along the ground to attack, escape, or hunt for food. With its Fury Swipes technique, Sandslash can attack two to five times in a row. Be sure not to leave this Pokémon out where someone can step on it. Ouch!

Pokédex Pick:
Although most Pokémon can understand people, each species has its own language. The language is made up of the Pokémon's own name. In the cartoon, Meowth is the only Pokémon that can speak a human language.

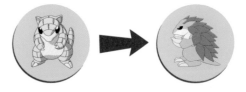

PRONUNCIATION:
NEE-DOOR-ANN

ELEMENT:
POISON

TYPE:
POISON PIN

HEIGHT:
1' 4"

WEIGHT:
15 LBS

TECHNIQUES:
GROWL, TACKLE,

OTHER TECHNIQUES:
**SCRATCH,
POISON STING,
TAIL WHIP,
BITE,
FURY SWIPES,
DOUBLE KICK**

GOOD AGAINST:
GRASS, BUG

BAD AGAINST:
**POISON, GROUND,
ROCK, GHOST**

EVOLUTION:
NORMAL

EVOLVES AT LEVEL:
16

The female Nidoran has small, poisonous barbs that make her very dangerous. Her horns may be smaller than a male Nidoran's spikes, but they are just as powerful.

Pokédex Pick:
COMMUNITY SERVICE:
Volunteer at Mr. Fuji's Abandoned Pokémon House in Lavender Town. Share your love with a Pokémon that doesn't have a trainer.

#30 NIDORINA

PRONUNCIATION:
NEE-DOOR-EE-NUH

ELEMENT:
POISON

TYPE:
POISON PIN

HEIGHT:
2' 7"

WEIGHT:
44 LBS

TECHNIQUES:
GROWL,
TACKLE,
SCRATCH

OTHER
TECHNIQUES:
POISON STING,
TAIL WHIP,
BITE,
FURY SWIPES,
DOUBLE KICK

GOOD AGAINST:
GRASS, BUG

BAD AGAINST:
POISON,
GROUND,
ROCK, GHOST

EVOLUTION:
MOON STONE

A Nidorina does not evolve by gaining more experience. You need to use a Moon Stone to turn her into a Nidoqueen. Because the female Nidorina's horns grow slowly, she likes to use her teeth and claws in battle instead.

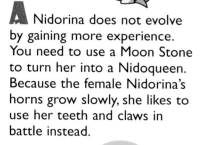

#31 NIDOQUEEN

PRONUNCIATION:
NEE-DOE-QUEEN

ELEMENT:
POISON/GROUND

TYPE:
DRILL

HEIGHT:
4' 3"

WEIGHT:
132 LBS

TECHNIQUES:
TACKLE,
SCRATCH,
TAIL WHIP

OTHER
TECHNIQUES:
POISON STING,
BODY SLAM

GOOD AGAINST:
ELECTRIC, FIRE

BAD AGAINST:
GROUND, GHOST

EVOLUTION:
MOON STONE

N idoqueen, on the other hand, favors her heavy but powerful tail. She likes to use her massive size for strong attacks like the Body Slam. The hard scales on Nidoqueen give her lots of protection.

PRONUNCIATION:
NEE-DOOR-ANN

ELEMENT:
POISON

TYPE:
POISON PIN

HEIGHT:
1' 8"

WEIGHT:
20 LBS

TECHNIQUES:
LEER, TACKLE

OTHER TECHNIQUES:
**HORN ATTACK,
POISON STING,
FOCUS ENERGY,
FURY ATTACK,
HORN DRILL,
DOUBLE KICK**

GOOD AGAINST:
GRASS, BUG

BAD AGAINST:
**POISON, GROUND,
ROCK, GHOST**

EVOLUTION:
NORMAL

EVOLVES AT LEVEL:
16

Nidoran males have ears that stiffen at any sign of danger. The barbs on their heads release a powerful poison.

#33 NIDORINO

PRONUNCIATION:
NEE-DOOR-EE-NO

ELEMENT:
POISON

TYPE:
POISON PIN

HEIGHT:
2' 11"

WEIGHT:
43 LBS

TECHNIQUES:
LEER, TACKLE, HORN ATTACK

OTHER TECHNIQUES:
POISON STING, FOCUS ENERGY, FURY ATTACK, HORN DRILL, DOUBLE KICK

GOOD AGAINST:
GRASS, BUG

BAD AGAINST:
POISON, GROUND, ROCK, GHOST

EVOLUTION:
MOON STONE

The horn on Nidorino's head contains a strong poison. At higher levels, its Horn Drill technique can defeat an enemy in seconds. Keep it away from small children and animals.

Pokédex Pick:
In battle, Nidorino often uses Focus Energy to increase its power before attacking. Use that pause to attack before it attacks your Pokémon.

#34 NIDOKING

PRONUNCIATION:
NEE-DOE-KING

ELEMENT:
POISON/GROUND

TYPE:
DRILL

HEIGHT:
4' 7"

WEIGHT:
137 LBS

TECHNIQUES:
TACKLE, HORN ATTACK, POISON STING

OTHER TECHNIQUES:
THRASH

GOOD AGAINST:
ELECTRIC, FIRE

BAD AGAINST:
GROUND, GHOST

EVOLUTION:
MOON STONE

Nidoking is a powerful warrior. He wraps his strong tail around his prey and crushes its bones.

The friendly and peaceful Clefairy is admired by many for its magical powers. You will have to search long and hard to find one, though. It is very rare. Its special Metronome technique allows it to attack in many different ways. Some believe that the Clefairy have formed their own society inside Mt. Moon where they pray to the Moon Stone. According to legend, the Stone fell from the Moon hundreds of years ago.

Pokédex Pick:

Elemental stones like the Fire, Water, Leaf, Thunder, and Moon Stones are needed to evolve some Pokémon. They are found in dungeons or at the Celadon City department store. The Moon Stone is the rarest. But did you know that there aren't enough elemental stones for the seventeen species of Pokémon that need them to evolve? Special stones are in short supply, so use 'em wisely.

PRONUNCIATION:
CLUH-FAIR-EE
ELEMENT:
NORMAL
TYPE:
FAIRY
HEIGHT:
2' 0"
WEIGHT:
17 LBS
TECHNIQUES:
POUND, GROWL
OTHER TECHNIQUES:
SING, DOUBLESLAP, MINIMIZE, METRONOME, DEFENSE CURL, LIGHT SCREEN
GOOD AGAINST:
NONE
BAD AGAINST:
ROCK
EVOLUTION:
MOON STONE

PRONUNCIATION:
CLUH-FAY-BULL

ELEMENT:
NORMAL

TYPE:
FAIRY

HEIGHT:
4' 3"

WEIGHT:
88 LBS

TECHNIQUES:
SING,
DOUBLESLAP,
MINIMIZE,
METRONOME

OTHER TECHNIQUES:
NONE

GOOD AGAINST:
NONE

BAD AGAINST:
ROCK

EVOLUTION:
MOON STONE

Clefable is one of the rarest Pokémon in the world. You will need to use a Moon Stone to turn a Clefairy into a Clefable. Once you do, your Clefable will not be able to learn any new techniques without special tools. You may want to make sure it knows a variety of techniques before you evolve it. Clefable is a very shy fairy that is hardly ever seen. It runs and hides the second it thinks people are around. You will need to be extra loving and gentle with this Pokémon to gain its trust.

PRONUNCIATION:
VULL-PICKS
ELEMENT:
FIRE
TYPE:
FOX
HEIGHT:
2' 0'
WEIGHT:
22 LBS
TECHNIQUES:
EMBER,
TAIL WHIP
OTHER TECHNIQUES:
QUICK ATTACK,
ROAR,
CONFUSE RAY,
FLAMETHROWER,
FIRE SPIN
GOOD AGAINST:
GRASS, ICE, BUG
BAD AGAINST:
FIRE, WATER, ROCK,
DRAGON
EVOLUTION:
FIRE STONE

A cute exterior hides inner strength. This fire Pokémon is extremely rare. As Vulpix grows older its tail splits at the tip. Vulpix likes to confuse its enemy. Then it uses the powerful flames of its Fire Spin technique to block an opponent from moving.

#38 NINETALES

PRONUNCIATION:
NINE-TAILS
ELEMENT:
FIRE
TYPE:
FOX
HEIGHT:
3' 7"
WEIGHT:
44 LBS
TECHNIQUES:
EMBER,
TAIL WHIP,
QUICK ATTACK,
ROAR
OTHER TECHNIQUES:
NONE
GOOD AGAINST:
GRASS, ICE, BUG
BAD AGAINST:
FIRE, WATER,
ROCK, DRAGON
EVOLUTION:
FIRE STONE

The only way to add a Ninetales to your Pokémon team is to carefully raise a Vulpix and then use a Fire Stone to evolve it. Ninetales is a very smart Pokémon that likes plotting revenge against its enemies. If you grab one of its tails, Ninetales may put a thousand-year curse on you!

#39 JIGGLYPUFF

PRONUNCIATION:
JIG-LEE-PUFF
ELEMENT:
NORMAL
TYPE:
BALLOON
HEIGHT:
1' 8"
WEIGHT:
12 LBS
TECHNIQUES:
SING

OTHER
TECHNIQUES:
**POUND,
DISABLE,
DEFENSE CURL,
DOUBLESLAP,
REST, BODY
SLAM,
DOUBLE EDGE**
GOOD AGAINST:
NONE
BAD AGAINST:
ROCK
EVOLUTION:
MOON STONE

Looks can be deceiving! Just because this Pokémon has big, friendly eyes and makes a cuddly, cute pet doesn't mean it can't fight. Jigglypuff's Sing attack can soothe even the toughest Pokémon into dreamland. Then it's time for a pounding as soon as they're snoozing. Jigglypuff are very rare, so if magical and mysterious Pokémon are your thing, take time to search the long grass outside Mt. Moon for this ball of fluff.

#40 WIGGLYTUFF

PRONUNCIATION:
WIG-LEE-TUFF
ELEMENT:
NORMAL
TYPE:
BALLOON
HEIGHT:
3' 3"
WEIGHT:
26 LBS
TECHNIQUES:
**SING, DISABLE,
DEFENSE CURL,
DOUBLESLAP**

OTHER
TECHNIQUES:
NONE
GOOD AGAINST:
NONE
BAD AGAINST:
ROCK
EVOLUTION:
MOON STONE

You don't want to mess with this big-eyed Pokémon. When it gets angry, Wigglytuff sucks in air and inflates its soft, rubbery body like a giant balloon. At supersize, it can scare off even the meanest enemies. How do you explain that to Mom and Dad?

#41 ZUBAT

PRONUNCIATION:
ZOO-BAT

ELEMENT:
POISON/FLYING

TYPE:
BAT

HEIGHT:
2' 7"

WEIGHT:
17 LBS

TECHNIQUES:
LEECH LIFE

OTHER
TECHNIQUES:
SUPERSONIC,
BITE,
CONFUSE RAY,
WING ATTACK,
HAZE

GOOD AGAINST:
GRASS, BUG,
FIGHTING

BAD AGAINST:
GROUND,
POISON, ROCK,
GHOST,
ELECTRIC

EVOLUTION:
NORMAL

EVOLVES AT LEVEL:
22

Zubat live in colonies — or groups — in dark places like caves and tunnels. They use ultrasonic waves — a built-in radar system — to move around in the dark and find enemies. Their Leech Life technique sucks the energy out of an opponent. Then their own energy increases.

#42 GOLBAT

PRONUNCIATION:
GOAL-BAT

ELEMENT:
POISON/FLYING

TYPE:
BAT

HEIGHT:
5' 3"

WEIGHT:
121 LBS

TECHNIQUES:
LEECH LIFE,
SCREECH, BITE,
CONFUSE RAY

OTHER
TECHNIQUES:
WING ATTACK,
HAZE

GOOD AGAINST:
GRASS, BUG,
FIGHTING

BAD AGAINST:
POISON, ROCK,
GHOST,
ELECTRIC

EVOLUTION:
NORMAL

The fully evolved Golbat also feeds on its victim's energy. Using its sharp fangs, Golbat can drain 48 cubic inches of blood per bite. Its Haze technique confuses an opponent so it can't tell if the Golbat is an enemy or a friend.

PRONUNCIATION:
ODD-ISH

ELEMENT:
GRASS/POISON

TYPE:
WEED

HEIGHT:
1' 8"

WEIGHT:
12 LBS

TECHNIQUES:
ABSORB

OTHER TECHNIQUES:
POISON POWDER, STUN SPORE, SLEEP POWDER, ACID, PETAL DANCE, SOLAR BEAM

GOOD AGAINST:
WATER

BAD AGAINST:
FIRE, POISON, FLYING, DRAGON, GHOST

EVOLUTION:
NORMAL

EVOLVES AT LEVEL:
21

Oddish is, well, odd. During the day, this weedlike Pokémon keeps its head buried in the ground. At night, it wanders around planting seeds and sprinkling pollen as it walks. It likes to poison or stun its enemy and then it drains its energy. At higher levels, this combo Grass/Poison Pokémon has many special abilities. Its Petal Dance hurts and confuses other Pokémon. Oddish uses Solar Beam to increase its own energy on its first turn so it can have an extra powerful attack on its second turn.

#44 GLOOM

PRONUNCIATION:
GLOOM

ELEMENT:
GRASS/POISON

TYPE:
WEED

HEIGHT:
2'7"

WEIGHT:
19 LBS

TECHNIQUES:
ABSORB,
POISON
POWDER,
STUN SPORE,
SLEEP POWDER

OTHER
TECHNIQUES:
ACID,
PETAL DANCE,
SOLAR BEAM

GOOD AGAINST:
WATER

BAD AGAINST:
FIRE, POISON,
FLYING,
DRAGON,
GHOST

EVOLUTION:
LEAF STONE

Like most Grass Pokémon, Gloom can't move very well. But it doesn't have to move with attacks like Poison Powder and Stun Spore. The liquid that oozes out of its mouth isn't drool. It's a nectar that Gloom uses to get the enemy to come closer. When Gloom feels as if it's in danger, it starts to smell — bad.

#45 VILEPLUME

PRONUNCIATION:
VILE-PLOOM

ELEMENT:
GRASS/POISON

TYPE:
FLOWER

HEIGHT:
3'11"

WEIGHT:
41 LBS

TECHNIQUES:
POISON
POWDER,
STUN SPORE,
SLEEP POWDER

OTHER
TECHNIQUES:
NONE

GOOD AGAINST:
WATER

BAD AGAINST:
FIRE, POISON,
FLYING,
DRAGON,
GHOST

EVOLUTION:
LEAF STONE

Once you've used a Leaf Stone to turn your Gloom into Vileplume, its big head will get heavy and hard to hold up.

#46 PARAS

PRONUNCIATION:
PAR-ISS

ELEMENT:
BUG/GRASS

TYPE:
MUSHROOM

HEIGHT:
1'0"

WEIGHT:
12 LBS

TECHNIQUES:
SCRATCH

OTHER TECHNIQUES:
STUN SPORE, LEECH LIFE, SPORE, SLASH, GROWTH

GOOD AGAINST:
PSYCHIC, WATER, GROUND, ROCK

BAD AGAINST:
GHOST, FLYING, FIGHTING, FIRE, POISON, BUG, DRAGON

EVOLUTION:
NORMAL

EVOLVES AT LEVEL:
24

Paras is a combo Bug/Grass Pokémon. It has insectlike claws and rare mushrooms on its back. Its relationship with the mushrooms is an example of symbiosis. The mushroomlike pods take nutrients from their Bug host. In return, the mushrooms shoot out clouds of Stun Spores to stun almost any opponent. When it isn't fighting, Paras burrows underground to suck tree roots.

#47 PARASECT

PRONUNCIATION:
PAR-I-SECT

ELEMENT:
BUG/GRASS

TYPE:
MUSHROOM

HEIGHT:
3'3"

WEIGHT:
65 LBS

TECHNIQUES:
SCRATCH, STUN SPORE, LEECH LIFE

OTHER TECHNIQUES:
SPORE, SLASH, GROWTH

GOOD AGAINST:
PSYCHIC, WATER, GROUND, ROCK

BAD AGAINST:
GHOST, FLYING, FIGHTING, FIRE, POISON, BUG, DRAGON

EVOLUTION:
NORMAL

By the time Paras has evolved into Parasect, the mushroom on its back has taken over its entire body. The giant mushroom is a good defense against enemies. Its Spore technique puts attackers to sleep. Parasect's mushroom can also be used to make magical potions. One potion makes all the Pokémon in the world stronger.

#48 VENONAT

PRONUNCIATION:
VENN-OH-NAT

ELEMENT:
BUG/POISON

TYPE:
INSECT

HEIGHT:
3' 3"

WEIGHT:
66 LBS

TECHNIQUES:
TACKLE,
DISABLE

OTHER TECHNIQUES:
POISON POWDER,
LEECH LIFE,
STUN SPORE,
PSYBEAM,
SLEEP POWDER,
PSYCHIC

GOOD AGAINST:
GRASS,
PSYCHIC, BUG

BAD AGAINST:
GHOST, FLYING,
FIGHTING, FIRE,
POISON, ROCK

EVOLUTION:
NORMAL

EVOLVES AT LEVEL:
31

The buglike Venonat eats insects and lives in the shadows and branches of tall trees. At night, it likes to fly near bright lights.

#49 VENOMOTH

PRONUNCIATION:
VENN-OH-MOTH

ELEMENT:
BUG/POISON

TYPE:
POISON MOTH

HEIGHT:
4' 11"

WEIGHT:
28 LBS

TECHNIQUES:
TACKLE,
DISABLE,
POISON POWDER,
LEECH LIFE,
STUN SPORE

OTHER TECHNIQUES:
PSYBEAM,
SLEEP POWDER,
PSYCHIC

GOOD AGAINST:
GRASS,
PSYCHIC, BUG

BAD AGAINST:
GROUND,
GHOST, FLYING,
FIGHTING, FIRE,
POISON, ROCK

EVOLUTION:
NORMAL

Venomoth has tons of powerful poisonous techniques. The dustlike scales covering Venomoth's wings are color coded to show the types of poisons it carries. Make sure you have a lot of Antidote in your first-aid kit.

#50 DIGLETT

PRONUNCIATION:
DIG-LIT
ELEMENT:
GROUND
TYPE:
MOLE
HEIGHT:
0'8"
WEIGHT:
2 LBS
TECHNIQUES:
SCRATCH
OTHER TECHNIQUES:
GROWL, DIG, SAND ATTACK, SLASH, EARTHQUAKE

GOOD AGAINST:
ELECTRIC, FLYING, FIRE, POISON, ROCK
BAD AGAINST:
GRASS, BUG
EVOLUTION:
NORMAL
EVOLVES AT LEVEL:
26

The hardest part of capturing a Diglett is getting it into your Poké Ball before it faints or runs away. Fighting a Diglett is good experience for a young Pokémon trainer. Diglett don't really change form, they join together in groups of three to become Dugtrio.

#51 DUGTRIO

PRONUNCIATION:
DUG-TREE-OH
ELEMENT:
GROUND
TYPE:
MOLE
HEIGHT:
2'4"
WEIGHT:
73 LBS
TECHNIQUES:
SCRATCH, GROWL, DIG, SAND ATTACK

OTHER TECHNIQUES:
SLASH, EARTHQUAKE
GOOD AGAINST:
FLYING, FIRE, POISON, ROCK
BAD AGAINST:
GRASS, BUG
EVOLUTION:
NORMAL

Dugtrio are harder to find than Diglett and are much more dangerous. But Dugtrio still focus on defense. They like to trigger huge earthquakes by digging up to sixty miles underground.

PRONUNCIATION:
ME-OUTH
ELEMENT:
NORMAL
TYPE:
SCRATCH CAT
HEIGHT:
I'4"
WEIGHT:
9 LBS
TECHNIQUES:
SCRATCH,
GROWL
OTHER TECHNIQUES:
BITE, PAY DAY,
SCREECH,
FURY SWIPES,
SLASH
GOOD AGAINST:
NONE
BAD AGAINST:
GHOST, ROCK
EVOLUTION:
NORMAL
EVOLVES AT LEVEL:
28

Meowth is ferocious. As a member of the evil Team Rocket, its mission is to help Jessie and James capture and mistreat rare Pokémon. It especially wants Pikachu. Meowth is ambitious and crafty, but it misses important details in its hurry to attack — which always leads to its own failure.

Meowth adores round objects. It will even wander the streets at night looking for change. Its Pay Day technique gives its trainer extra money after each victory.

Pokédex Pick:
In the Pokémon cartoon, Meowth is the only Pokémon that can speak a human language. Meowth's motto is, "I'm the top cat around here!"

PRONUNCIATION:
PURR-SHIN
ELEMENT:
NORMAL
TYPE:
CLASSY CAT
HEIGHT:
3' 3"
WEIGHT:
71 LBS
TECHNIQUES:
SCRATCH, GROWL, BITE, PAY DAY, SCREECH
OTHER TECHNIQUES:
FURY SWIPES, SLASH
GOOD AGAINST:
NONE
BAD AGAINST:
ROCK
EVOLUTION:
NORMAL

Persian are very clever and powerful. They use Growl to lower an opponent's attack power before attacking with their own teeth and claws. They have beautiful fur that is admired by many people.

Pokédex Pick:
Giovanni, diabolical mastermind behind the evil Team Rocket, pampers his purring Persian pet.

#54 PSYDUCK

PRONUNCIATION:
SYE-DUCK

ELEMENT:
WATER

TYPE:
DUCK

HEIGHT:
2' 7"

WEIGHT:
43 LBS

TECHNIQUES:
SCRATCH

OTHER TECHNIQUES:
TAIL WHIP, DISABLE, CONFUSION, FURY SWIPES, HYDRO PUMP

GOOD AGAINST:
FIRE, GROUND, ROCK

BAD AGAINST:
WATER, ELECTRIC, GRASS, DRAGON

EVOLUTION:
NORMAL

EVOLVES AT LEVEL:
33

Psy aye! Ay! Psyduck uses the mysterious power of its mind to hypnotize its enemy with an empty, spooky stare. When its own headaches get superstrong and Psyduck's mind is about to burst, it lets loose an overload of mental energy. Aside from this, Psyduck can be clumsy on land.

Pokédex Pick:

Misty — a Pokémon trainer who likes to collect Water Pokémon — has a Psyduck of her own. When Misty calls for another one of her Water Pokémon to come out of its Poké Ball, Psyduck likes to pop out instead of the other Pokémon.

#55 GOLDUCK

PRONUNCIATION:
GOAL-DUCK
ELEMENT:
WATER
TYPE:
DUCK
HEIGHT:
5' 7"
WEIGHT:
169 LBS
TECHNIQUES:
**SCRATCH,
TAIL WHIP, DISABLE**
OTHER TECHNIQUES:
**CONFUSION,
FURY SWIPES,
HYDRO PUMP**
GOOD AGAINST:
FIRE, GROUND, ROCK
BAD AGAINST:
**WATER, ELECTRIC,
GRASS, DRAGON**
EVOLUTION:
NORMAL

Golduck is a very elegant Pokémon. It is a graceful fighter both on land and in the water. Golduck enjoys swimming by lakeshores. It looks surprisingly similar to the Japanese sea monster, Kappa.

Pokédex Pick:
PARTY TIME:
The S.S. *Anne* in Vermillion City is a party boat. It celebrates Pokémon every day!

#56 MANKEY

PRONUNCIATION:
MANK-EE
ELEMENT:
FIGHTING
TYPE:
PIG MONKEY
HEIGHT:
1' 8"
WEIGHT:
62 LBS
TECHNIQUES:
SCRATCH, LEER
OTHER TECHNIQUES:
KARATE CHOP,
FURY ATTACK,
FOCUS ENERGY,
SEISMIC TOSS,
THRASH
GOOD AGAINST:
NORMAL, ICE,
ROCK
BAD AGAINST:
POISON,
FLYING,
PSYCHIC, BUG
EVOLUTION:
NORMAL
EVOLVES AT LEVEL:
28

It doesn't take much to get Mankey angry. It can be calm one minute and hopping mad the next. Known for its superior footwork, Mankey also packs a powerful punch. As a Fighting Pokémon, it is quicker and more agile than most Pokémon. It can even easily avoid another Pokémon's special techniques.

#57 PRIMEAPE

PRONUNCIATION:
PRIME-APE
ELEMENT:
FIGHTING
TYPE:
PIG MONKEY
HEIGHT:
3' 3"
WEIGHT:
71 LBS
TECHNIQUES:
SCRATCH, LEER,
KARATE CHOP,
FURY ATTACK,
FOCUS ENERGY
OTHER TECHNIQUES:
SEISMIC TOSS,
THRASH
GOOD AGAINST:
NORMAL,
ICE, ROCK
BAD AGAINST:
POISON,
FLYING,
PSYCHIC, BUG
EVOLUTION:
NORMAL

Primeape won't give up a chase until it has caught its enemy. If you make eye contact with this bad-tempered ape, get ready to run for your life! Its Karate Chop technique is impressive.

#58 GROWLITHE

PRONUNCIATION:
GROWL-ITH

ELEMENT:
FIRE

TYPE:
PUPPY

HEIGHT:
2' 4"

WEIGHT:
42 LBS

TECHNIQUES:
BITE, ROAR

OTHER TECHNIQUES:
EMBER, LEER, TAKE DOWN,
AGILITY, FLAMETHROWER

GOOD AGAINST:
GRASS, ICE, BUG

BAD AGAINST:
FIRE, WATER, ROCK, DRAGON

EVOLUTION:
FIRE STONE

Growlithe, the puppy Pokémon, is very rare. Be careful when fighting it. It is way too protective of its territory and its owner. It will bark and bite to scare away intruders.

#59 ARCANINE

PRONUNCIATION:
AR-KUH-NINE

ELEMENT:
FIRE

TYPE:
LEGENDARY

HEIGHT:
6' 3"

WEIGHT:
342 LBS

TECHNIQUES:
ROAR, EMBER, LEER, TAKE DOWN

OTHER TECHNIQUES:
NONE

GOOD AGAINST:
GRASS, ICE, BUG

BAD AGAINST:
FIRE, WATER, ROCK, DRAGON

EVOLUTION:
FIRE STONE

Arcanine's beauty has been admired for centuries. It runs so quickly and easily it looks like it's flying. Arcanine makes a loyal pet, but be sure to train it well or it may bite any friends or family members who get too close to you.

PRONUNCIATION:
POL-EE-WAG

ELEMENT:
WATER

TYPE:
TADPOLE

HEIGHT:
2' 0"

WEIGHT:
27 LBS

TECHNIQUES:
BUBBLE

OTHER TECHNIQUES:
HYPNOSIS, WATER GUN, DOUBLESLAP, BODY SLAM, AMNESIA, HYDRO PUMP

GOOD AGAINST:
FIRE, GROUND, ROCK

BAD AGAINST:
WATER, ELECTRIC, GRASS, DRAGON

EVOLUTION:
NORMAL

EVOLVES AT LEVEL:
25

With newly grown legs and no arms for balance, Poliwag has a hard time standing and walking. Swimming seems to be its thing.

Pokédex Pick:
When Poliwag evolves into Poliwhirl, the swirl on its stomach changes direction.

#61 POLIWHIRL

PRONUNCIATION:
POL-EE-WURL

ELEMENT:
WATER

TYPE:
TADPOLE

HEIGHT:
3' 3"

WEIGHT:
44 LBS

TECHNIQUES:
BUBBLE,
HYPNOSIS,
WATER GUN

**OTHER
TECHNIQUES:**
DOUBLESLAP,

BODY SLAM,
AMNESIA,
HYDRO PUMP

GOOD AGAINST:
FIRE, GROUND,
ROCK

BAD AGAINST:
WATER,
ELECTRIC,
GRASS,
DRAGON

EVOLUTION:
WATER STONE

Once Poliwag has evolved into Poliwhirl it can live in or out of the water. Once out of the water, it sweats to keep its body slimy. It uses a variety of mind powers, like Amnesia, to make it more powerful.

#62 POLIWRATH

PRONUNCIATION:
POL-EE-RATH

ELEMENT:
WATER/
FIGHTING

TYPE:
TADPOLE

HEIGHT:
4' 3"

WEIGHT:
119 LBS

TECHNIQUES:
DOUBLESLAP,
BODY SLAM,
HYPNOSIS,
WATER GUN

**OTHER
TECHNIQUES:**
NONE

GOOD AGAINST:
FIRE, GROUND,
ROCK, NORMAL,
ICE

BAD AGAINST:
WATER,
ELECTRIC,
GRASS,
DRAGON,
GHOST, POISON,
FLYING,
PSYCHIC, BUG

EVOLUTION:
WATER STONE

Poliwrath is an outstanding swimmer. Its specialties are the front crawl and the breast-stroke. Once you evolve it using the Water Stone, Poliwrath takes on more Fighting charac-teristics, like Body Slam. But it can still use Hypnosis to soothe an enemy to sleep. Maybe Poliwrath will hypnotize you into letting it out of its Poké Ball more often.

PRONUNCIATION:
AB-RUH
ELEMENT:
PSYCHIC
TYPE:
PSYCHIC
HEIGHT:
2' 11"
WEIGHT:
43 LBS
TECHNIQUES:
TELEPORT
OTHER TECHNIQUES:
NONE
GOOD AGAINST:
FIGHTING, POISON
BAD AGAINST:
PSYCHIC
EVOLUTION:
NORMAL
EVOLVES AT LEVEL:
16

Abra's ability to read minds could come in very handy. It can sense danger and teleport (or move) itself — and you — to another place. Abra can't actually attack, but when you can escape bullies this easily, why bother? It also needs tons of rest — up to eighteen hours of sleep a day! But Abra can still use its brainwaves to move things around in its sleep. An Abra makes a good ally. To capture it, try paralyzing it before it can run away.

#64 KADABRA

PRONUNCIATION:
KAH-DA-BRUH

ELEMENT:
PSYCHIC

TYPE:
PSYCHIC

HEIGHT:
4' 3"

WEIGHT:
125 LBS

TECHNIQUES:
TELEPORT,
CONFUSION

OTHER TECHNIQUES:
DISABLE,
PSYBEAM,
RECOVER,
PSYCHIC,
REFLECT

GOOD AGAINST:
FIGHTING,
POISON

BAD AGAINST:
PSYCHIC

EVOLUTION:
TRADE

Like Abra, Kadabra likes to use its strong mind instead of its strong body to win competitions. It sends out special brainwaves that give headaches to anyone who gets too close.

#65 ALAKAZAM

PRONUNCIATION:
AL-UH-KUH-ZAM

ELEMENT:
PSYCHIC

TYPE:
PSYCHIC

HEIGHT:
4' 11"

WEIGHT:
106 LBS

TECHNIQUES:
TELEPORT,
CONFUSION

OTHER TECHNIQUES:
DISABLE,
PSYBEAM,
RECOVER,
PSYCHIC,
REFLECT

GOOD AGAINST:
FIGHTING,
POISON

BAD AGAINST:
PSYCHIC

EVOLUTION:
TRADE

Alakazam have amazingly powerful brains. They're smarter than a supercomputer! With an I.Q. of 5,000, Alakazam is a genius! Maybe, if you're very nice to it, Alakazam will help you with your homework.

#66 MACHOP

PRONUNCIATION:
MAH-CHOP

ELEMENT:
FIGHTING

TYPE:
SUPERPOWER

HEIGHT:
2' 7"

WEIGHT:
43 LBS

TECHNIQUES:
KARATE CHOP

OTHER TECHNIQUES:
LOW KICK, LEER,

FOCUS ENERGY, SEISMIC TOSS, SUBMISSION

GOOD AGAINST:
NORMAL, ICE, ROCK

BAD AGAINST:
POISON, FLYING, PSYCHIC, BUG

EVOLUTION:
TRADE

EVOLVES AT LEVEL:
28

Machop may be small, but it packs a lot of power. It loves to study all types of martial arts, like karate, to get stronger. It is very quick and mobile like a Mankey and can even avoid most special techniques. It's also one of the most intelligent Pokémon. Machop makes a loyal companion and great teacher.

#67 MACHOKE

PRONUNCIATION:
MAH-CHOKE

ELEMENT:
FIGHTING

TYPE:
SUPERPOWER

HEIGHT:
4' 1"

WEIGHT:
155 LBS

TECHNIQUES:
KARATE CHOP, LOW KICK, LEER

OTHER TECHNIQUES:
FOCUS ENERGY, SEISMIC TOSS, SUBMISSION

GOOD AGAINST:
NORMAL, ICE, ROCK

BAD AGAINST:
GHOST, POISON, FLYING, PSYCHIC, BUG

EVOLUTION:
TRADE

Machoke, on the other hand, likes its own body way too much. Sometimes it's too busy looking at itself in the mirror to train. Plus, Machoke is so strong, it has to wear a power-save belt to control its movements.

PRONUNCIATION:
MAH-CHAMP
ELEMENT:
FIGHTING
TYPE:
SUPERPOWER
HEIGHT:
5' 3"
WEIGHT:
287 LBS
TECHNIQUES:
**KARATE CHOP,
LOW KICK, LEER**
OTHER TECHNIQUES:
**FOCUS ENERGY,
SEISMIC TOSS,
SUBMISSION**
GOOD AGAINST:
NORMAL, ICE, ROCK
BAD AGAINST:
**POISON, FLYING,
PSYCHIC, BUG**
EVOLUTION:
TRADE

Machamp is definitely the strongest of the three evolutions. It has to be traded before it can evolve, but it doesn't mind. This Pokémon is all about fighting, and the extra arms are a big help. Machamp uses its huge muscles to throw powerful punches that can send a challenger to the Moon! It may not be the easiest Pokémon to keep in a Poké Ball, but Machamp would make an excellent bodyguard.

#69 BELLSPROUT

PRONUNCIATION:
BELL-SPROUT

ELEMENT:
GRASS/POISON

TYPE:
FLOWER

HEIGHT:
2' 4"

WEIGHT:
9 LBS

TECHNIQUES:
VINE WHIP, GROWTH

OTHER TECHNIQUES:
WRAP,
POISON POWDER,
SLEEP POWDER,
STUN SPORE, ACID,
RAZOR LEAF, SLAM

GOOD AGAINST:
WATER

BAD AGAINST:
FIRE, POISON,
FLYING, DRAGON,
GHOST

EVOLUTION:
NORMAL

EVOLVES AT LEVEL:
21

Bellsprout are plant Pokémon that trap and eat bugs, like a Venus flytrap. Their roots dig under the dirt to soak up needed moisture. If you're thinking about collecting a wild Bellsprout, use your most powerful technique before it has a chance to use Growth technique against you.

#70 WEEPINBELL

PRONUNCIATION:
WEEP-IN-BELL

ELEMENT:
GRASS/POISON

TYPE:
FLYCATCHER

HEIGHT:
3' 3"

WEIGHT:
14 LBS

TECHNIQUES:
VINE WHIP,
GROWTH, WRAP,
POISON POWDER,
SLEEP POWDER

OTHER TECHNIQUES:
STUN SPORE,
ACID,
RAZOR LEAF,
SLAM

GOOD AGAINST:
WATER

BAD AGAINST:
FIRE, POISON,
FLYING,
DRAGON, GHOST

EVOLUTION:
LEAF STONE

Like its cousin Bellsprout, Weepinbell likes to start off a good battle with its Growth technique and follow through with a little Poison Powder. Then all it takes is one spray of Acid to finish the fight.

#71 VICTREEBEL

PRONUNCIATION:
VICK-TREE-BELL

ELEMENT:
GRASS/POISON

TYPE:
FLYCATCHER

HEIGHT:
5' 7"

WEIGHT:
34 LBS

TECHNIQUES:
WRAP, POISON
POWDER,
SLEEP POWDER

OTHER TECHNIQUES:
NONE

GOOD AGAINST:
WATER

BAD AGAINST:
FIRE, POISON,
FLYING,
DRAGON,
GHOST

EVOLUTION:
LEAF STONE

If you happen to have a Leaf Stone, you may be able to evolve a Victreebel. According to rumor, Victreebel live in huge colonies or groups deep in the heart of the jungle.

#72 TENTACOOL

PRONUNCIATION:
TENT-UH-COOL

ELEMENT:
WATER/POISON

TYPE:
JELLYFISH

HEIGHT:
2' 11"

WEIGHT:
100 LBS

TECHNIQUES:
ACID

OTHER TECHNIQUES:
SUPERSONIC, WRAP, POISON STING, WATER GUN, CONSTRICT, BARRIER, SCREECH, HYDRO PUMP

GOOD AGAINST:
FIRE, BUG

BAD AGAINST:
WATER, ELECTRIC, DRAGON, POISON, GHOST

EVOLUTION:
NORMAL

EVOLVES AT LEVEL:
30

Tentacool's favorite pastime is floating in warm, shallow water. So if you live near a lake and the thermometer reads a constant 78°, this is the Pokémon for you! The beautiful red spot on a Tentacool's head is called the "ruby of the sea." Tentacool may be beautiful, but watch out for those stingers!

Pokédex Pick:
Tentacruel and Tentacool once took over all the ships in the harbor of Porta Vista city because a local millionaire — Nastina — tried to destroy their home.

PRONUNCIATION:
TENT-UH-CROOL

ELEMENT:
WATER/POISON

TYPE:
JELLYFISH

HEIGHT:
5' 3"

WEIGHT:
121 LBS

TECHNIQUES:
ACID, SUPERSONIC, WRAP, POISON STING, WATER GUN, CONSTRICT

OTHER TECHNIQUES:
BARRIER, SCREECH, HYDRO PUMP

GOOD AGAINST:
FIRE, BUG

BAD AGAINST:
WATER, ELECTRIC, DRAGON, POISON, GHOST

EVOLUTION:
NORMAL

Tentacruel's nickname is, "The gangster of the sea." That may have something to do with the dozen or so new stinger-tipped tentacles it grows during evolution. Its sting is vicious! It likes to keep its tentacles short, except when hunting. Then the tentacles extend to trap and stun unsuspecting prey.

PRONUNCIATION:
GEE-OH-DOOD
ELEMENT:
ROCK/GROUND
TYPE:
ROCK
HEIGHT:
1' 4"
WEIGHT:
44 LBS
TECHNIQUES:
TACKLE
OTHER TECHNIQUES:
DEFENSE CURL,
ROCK THROW,
SELF DESTRUCT,
HARDEN,
EARTHQUAKE,
EXPLOSION
GOOD AGAINST:
FIRE, ICE, ELECTRIC,
POISON, ROCK,
FLYING
BAD AGAINST:
FIGHTING, GROUND,
GRASS
EVOLUTION:
NORMAL
EVOLVES AT LEVEL:
25

Geodude rocks! It hangs out in fields and mountains. But unless you bother it, Geodude probably won't move. In fact, most passersby just think it's a rock or boulder. Not much fun — unless you're into the pet rock thing. Paint it multicolors and see if Geodude notices. Watch out, though. Geodude's rocklike skin makes it hard to attack — and almost impossible to capture.

PRONUNCIATION:
GRAV-EL-ER
ELEMENT:
ROCK/GROUND
TYPE:
ROCK
HEIGHT:
3' 3"
WEIGHT:
232 LBS
TECHNIQUES:
TACKLE,
DEFENSE CURL,
ROCK THROW,
SELF DESTRUCT

OTHER TECHNIQUES:
HARDEN,
EARTHQUAKE,
EXPLOSION
GOOD AGAINST:
FIRE, ICE,
ELECTRIC,
POISON, ROCK,
FLYING
BAD AGAINST:
FIGHTING,
GROUND, GRASS
EVOLUTION:
TRADE

Graveler moves by rolling down hills. It will also roll right over anything that gets in its way — without even slowing down or changing direction. As it evolves, Graveler's rocky skin grows layers of jagged scales.

#76 GOLEM

PRONUNCIATION:
GOAL-UM
ELEMENT:
ROCK/GROUND
TYPE:
MEGATON
HEIGHT:
4' 7"
WEIGHT:
622 LBS
TECHNIQUES:
TACKLE,
DEFENSE CURL,
ROCK THROW,
SELF DESTRUCT

OTHER TECHNIQUES:
HARDEN,
EARTHQUAKE,
EXPLOSION
GOOD AGAINST:
FIRE, ICE,
ELECTRIC,
POISON, ROCK,
FLYING
BAD AGAINST:
FIGHTING,
GROUND,
GRASS
EVOLUTION:
TRADE

Golem's massive size and great strength make it hard to collect. Dynamite blasts don't even hurt it. Golem are easier to spot in fields and mountains than Geodude or Graveler. It's hard to get Golem angry, but watch out if you do! They are fierce fighters when provoked. Once a year, Golem shed their bedrock shell and get even bigger. You'll have to trade a Graveler with a friend in order to evolve it into a Golem.

PRONUNCIATION:
PO-*NEE*-TUH

ELEMENT:
FIRE

TYPE:
FIRE HORSE

HEIGHT:
3' 3"

WEIGHT:
66 LBS

TECHNIQUES:
EMBER

OTHER TECHNIQUES:
TAIL WHIP, STOMP,
GROWL, FIRE SPIN,
TAKE DOWN, AGILITY

GOOD AGAINST:
GRASS, ICE, BUG

BAD AGAINST:
FIRE, WATER,
ROCK, DRAGON

EVOLUTION:
NORMAL

EVOLVES AT LEVEL:
40

Ponyta make great racers. So if you like to ride horseback at high speed, this is the Pokémon for you. They're great jumpers, too — even over water. Their mane is made of flames, but Ponyta would never burn anyone they truly trusted. Their hooves are ten times harder than diamonds, and they can trample anything flat as a pancake in seconds.

Pokédex Pick:

Famous Pokémon breeder Lara Larame raises an entire ranch full of Ponyta. According to popular opinion, the Ponyta she trains are some of the strongest around.

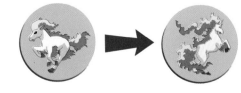

PRONUNCIATION:
RAP-I-DASH

ELEMENT:
FIRE

TYPE:
FIRE HORSE

HEIGHT:
5' 7"

WEIGHT:
209 LBS

TECHNIQUES:
EMBER, TAIL WHIP,
STOMP, GROWL,
FIRE SPIN

OTHER TECHNIQUES:
TAKE DOWN, AGILITY

GOOD AGAINST:
GRASS, ICE, BUG

BAD AGAINST:
FIRE, WATER, ROCK,
DRAGON

EVOLUTION:
NORMAL

The name says it all. This horselike Pokémon is fast! With its super speed, Rapidash can strike an opponent several times in a row. It's also extremely competitive. Rapidash will chase anything that moves in the hopes of racing it. Catch it if you can!

PRONUNCIATION:
SLOW-POKE

ELEMENT:
WATER/PSYCHIC

TYPE:
DOPEY

HEIGHT:
3' 11"

WEIGHT:
79 LBS

TECHNIQUES:
CONFUSION

OTHER TECHNIQUES:
DISABLE,
HEAD BUTT, GROWL,
WATER GUN,
AMNESIA, PSYCHIC

GOOD AGAINST:
FIRE, GROUND,
ROCK, FIGHTING,
POISON

BAD AGAINST:
DRAGON, WATER,
ELECTRIC, GRASS,
PSYCHIC

EVOLUTION:
NORMAL

EVOLVES AT LEVEL:
37

Unlike Ponyta and Rapidash, Slowpoke does NOT like to move. Everything about it is SLOW, SLOW, SLOW . . . and dopey. It takes Slowpoke an average of five seconds to realize it's in pain! To evolve a Slowpoke just dip its tail in the ocean and wait for a Shellder to bite. When it does — instant Slowbro! If you're gifted with patience, this is the Pokémon for you.

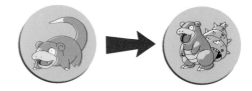

PRONUNCIATION:
SLOW-BRO
ELEMENT:
WATER/PSYCHIC
TYPE:
HERMIT CRAB
HEIGHT:
5' 3"
WEIGHT:
173 LBS
TECHNIQUES:
**CONFUSION,
DISABLE,
HEAD BUTT,
GROWL, WATER GUN,
WITHDRAW**
OTHER TECHNIQUES:
AMNESIA, PSYCHIC
GOOD AGAINST:
**FIRE, GROUND,
ROCK, FIGHTING,
POISON**
BAD AGAINST:
**DRAGON, WATER,
ELECTRIC, GRASS,
PSYCHIC**
EVOLUTION:
NORMAL

Slowbro is slow mentally and physically. But it is cute and lovable, and Slowbro's luck and instincts are good. Overall, a good pet — although teaching it a new technique may be frustrating.

#81 MAGNEMITE

PRONUNCIATION:
MAG-NUH-MITE

ELEMENT:
ELECTRIC

TYPE:
MAGNET

HEIGHT:
1' 0"

WEIGHT:
13 LBS

TECHNIQUES:
TACKLE

OTHER TECHNIQUES:
SONIC BOOM,
THUNDER-
SHOCK,
SUPERSONIC,
THUNDER WAVE,
SWIFT,
SCREECH

GOOD AGAINST:
WATER, FLYING

BAD AGAINST:
ELECTRIC,
GRASS,
DRAGON

EVOLUTION:
NORMAL

EVOLVES AT LEVEL:
30

Magnemite the mighty. Its Thunder Wave and other shocking techniques are almost unbeatable. Magnemite appears out of nowhere and has a mysterious antigravity skill that keeps it floating in the air. Magnemite are also good at finding lost paper clips and other small metal objects.

#82 MAGNETON

PRONUNCIATION:
MAG-NUH-TUN

ELEMENT:
ELECTRIC

TYPE:
MAGNET

HEIGHT:
3' 3"

WEIGHT:
132 LBS

TECHNIQUES:
TACKLE,
SONIC BOOM,
THUNDER-
SHOCK,
SUPERSONIC

OTHER TECHNIQUES:
THUNDER WAVE,
SWIFT, SCREECH

GOOD AGAINST:
WATER, FLYING

BAD AGAINST:
ELECTRIC,
GRASS,
DRAGON

EVOLUTION:
NORMAL

Three Magnemite join together to form one Magneton. When dark sunspots appear on the Sun, Magneton attack more often.

PRONUNCIATION:
FAR-FETCHT
ELEMENT:
NORMAL/FLYING
TYPE:
WILD DUCK
HEIGHT:
2' 7"
WEIGHT:
33 LBS
TECHNIQUES:
PECK,
SAND ATTACK
OTHER TECHNIQUES:
LEER,
FURY ATTACK,
SWORDS DANCE,
AGILITY, SLASH
GOOD AGAINST:
GRASS, FIGHTING,
BUG
BAD AGAINST:
ROCK, ELECTRIC
EVOLUTION:
NONE

Farfetch'd is one of a kind. With its Swords Dance technique, this ducklike Pokémon uses sprigs of green onions as miniswords. This is the Pokémon for trainers who like to stand out in a crowd. Unfortunately, Farfetch'd are almost extinct because some people think they make a delicious meal when served with leeks. Never fear, a trader in Vermillion City will give you Farfetch'd in exchange for a Spearow.

#84 DODUO

PRONUNCIATION:
DOE-DOO-OH

ELEMENT:
NORMAL/FLYING

TYPE:
TWIN BIRD

HEIGHT:
4' 7"

WEIGHT:
86 LBS

TECHNIQUES:
PECK

OTHER
TECHNIQUES:
FURY ATTACK,
DRILL PECK,
RAGE,
TRI ATTACK,
GROWL, AGILITY

GOOD AGAINST:
GRASS,
FIGHTING, BUG

BAD AGAINST:
ROCK,
ELECTRIC

EVOLUTION:
NORMAL

EVOLVES AT LEVEL:
31

Doduo can't fly very well. But they're so fast, they don't need to. Doduo have giant feet that leave huge footprints in the ground.

#85 DODRIO

PRONUNCIATION:
DOE-DREE-OH

ELEMENT:
NORMAL/FLYING

TYPE:
TRIPLE BIRD

HEIGHT:
5' 11"

WEIGHT:
188 LBS

TECHNIQUES:
PECK, GROWL,
FURY ATTACK,
DRILL PECK

OTHER
TECHNIQUES:
RAGE,
TRI ATTACK,
AGILITY

GOOD AGAINST:
GRASS,
FIGHTING, BUG

BAD AGAINST:
ROCK,
ELECTRIC

EVOLUTION:
NORMAL

Three heads are better than one! Dodrio has one head for joy, one for sorrow, and another for anger. Plus, three heads means three brains. And that makes Dodrio supersmart. It invents complicated plans to win battles. When does Dodrio find time to rest? While two heads sleep, one stays awake!

#86 SEEL

PRONUNCIATION:
SEEL
ELEMENT:
WATER
TYPE:
SEA LION

HEIGHT:
3' 7"
WEIGHT:
198 LBS
TECHNIQUES:
HEAD BUTT

OTHER
TECHNIQUES:
**AURORA BEAM,
REST,
TAKE DOWN,
ICE BEAM,
GROWL**
GOOD AGAINST:
**FIRE, GROUND,
ROCK**
BAD AGAINST:
**WATER,
ELECTRIC,
GRASS,
DRAGON**
EVOLUTION:
NORMAL
EVOLVES AT LEVEL:
34

Brrrrrrrrrrrrrrrr! Seel lives in the freezing-cold Arctic and uses the hard horn on its head to smash through thick ice. If you can stand the cold, Seel is a lovable friend.

#87 DEWGONG

PRONUNCIATION:
DOO-GONG
ELEMENT:
WATER/ICE
TYPE:
SEA LION
HEIGHT:
5' 7"
WEIGHT:
265 LBS
TECHNIQUES:
**HEAD BUTT,
GROWL**

OTHER
TECHNIQUES:
**AURORA BEAM,
REST,
TAKE DOWN,
ICE BEAM**
GOOD AGAINST:
**GROUND, ROCK,
FLYING**
BAD AGAINST:
**WATER,
ELECTRIC, ICE**
EVOLUTION:
NORMAL

Dewgong stores thermal energy from the sun in its body. It swims steadily and with great speed even in severely cold waters. With its special Rest technique, Dewgong can bring itself back to full health — but then it will need to skip two turns in battle!

#88 GRIMER

PRONUNCIATION:
GRIME-ER
ELEMENT:
POISON
TYPE:
SLUDGE
HEIGHT:
2' 11"
WEIGHT:
66 LBS
TECHNIQUES:
POUND,
DISABLE
**OTHER
TECHNIQUES:**
POISON GAS,
MINIMIZE,
SLUDGE,
HARDEN,
SCREECH,
ACID ARMOR
GOOD AGAINST:
GRASS, BUG
BAD AGAINST:
POISON,
GROUND, ROCK,
GHOST
EVOLUTION:
NORMAL
EVOLVES AT LEVEL:
38

Grimer and Muk love dirt and slime. So it's not surprising that they tend to hang around with Team Rocket. Grimer can actually be used as a natural pollution-processing plant because it likes to suck up the polluted sludge that is pumped out of factories and gym lockers.

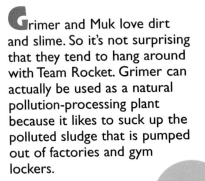

#89 MUK

PRONUNCIATION:
MUCK
ELEMENT:
POISON
TYPE:
SLUDGE
HEIGHT:
3' 11"
WEIGHT:
66 LBS
TECHNIQUES:
POUND,
DISABLE,
POISON GAS,
MINIMIZE,
SLUDGE
**OTHER
TECHNIQUES:**
HARDEN,
SCREECH,
ACID ARMOR
GOOD AGAINST:
GRASS, BUG
BAD AGAINST:
POISON,
GROUND, ROCK,
GHOST
EVOLUTION:
NORMAL

The slime on Muk's body is so toxic, even its footprints are poisonous!

Pokédex Pick:
Keeping too many Grimer and Muk in one place can be a hazard to your plumbing. They are so slimy, they once caused a power failure by clogging up the pipes used to pump water into a power plant!

#90 SHELLDER

PRONUNCIATION:
SHELL-DER
ELEMENT:
WATER
TYPE:
BIVALVE
HEIGHT:
1' 0"
WEIGHT:
9 LBS
TECHNIQUES:
TACKLE,
WITHDRAW

OTHER TECHNIQUES:
SUPERSONIC,
CLAMP,
AURORA BEAM,
LEER, ICE BEAM
GOOD AGAINST:
FIRE, GROUND,
ROCK
BAD AGAINST:
WATER,
ELECTRIC,
GRASS,
DRAGON
EVOLUTION:
WATER STONE

Shellder can be a little mischievous. It likes to tease its opponents during battle by sticking out its tongue and spitting in their eyes between attacks. Its hard shell is the best type of protection. Nothing gets past it!

#91 CLOYSTER

PRONUNCIATION:
CLOY-STIR
ELEMENT:
WATER/ICE
TYPE:
BIVALVE
HEIGHT:
4' 11"
WEIGHT:
292 LBS
TECHNIQUES:
WITHDRAW,
SUPERSONIC,
CLAMP,
AURORA BEAM

OTHER TECHNIQUES:
SPIKE CANNON
GOOD AGAINST:
GROUND, ROCK,
FLYING
BAD AGAINST:
WATER,
ELECTRIC, ICE
EVOLUTION:
WATER STONE

Cloyster is much more serious about competition than Shellder. It uses its Spike Cannon technique to hit its enemy up to five times in a row. Its shell is so protective, not even a bomb could get it open. No one has ever seen Cloyster's soft innerbody.

#92 GASTLY

PRONUNCIATION:
GAST-LEE
ELEMENT:
GHOST/POISON
TYPE:
GAS
HEIGHT:
4' 3"
WEIGHT:
0.2 LBS
TECHNIQUES:
LICK,
CONFUSE RAY,
NIGHT SHADE

OTHER TECHNIQUES:
HYPNOSIS,
DREAM EATER
GOOD AGAINST:
PSYCHIC,
GRASS, BUG
BAD AGAINST:
POISON,
GROUND, ROCK,
GHOST
EVOLUTION:
NORMAL
EVOLVES AT LEVEL:
25

Gastly and Haunter are part of a trio of poisonous Ghost Pokémon that reek havoc in the eerie Pokémon Tower. No Pokémon in existence has an advantage over Ghost Pokémon like Gastly and Haunter. Gastly is made of gas, so it's almost invisible. It can surround opponents and put them to sleep without them even noticing.

#93 HAUNTER

PRONUNCIATION:
HAWN-TER
ELEMENT:
GHOST/POISON
TYPE:
GAS
HEIGHT:
5' 3"
WEIGHT:
0.2 LBS
TECHNIQUES:
LICK,
CONFUSE RAY,
NIGHT SHADE
OTHER TECHNIQUES:
HYPNOSIS,

DREAM EATER
GOOD AGAINST:
PSYCHIC,
GRASS, BUG
BAD AGAINST:
POISON,
GROUND, ROCK,
GHOST
EVOLUTION:
TRADE

The true nature of Gastly and Haunter is shrouded in mystery. Are they spooky spectres or lonely Pokémon that just want to play?

Pokédex Pick:
It is rumored that Gastly have dedicated themselves to keeping alive the old, scary legends people have forgotten over the years.

PRONUNCIATION:
GANG-ARE

ELEMENT:
GHOST/POISON

TYPE:
SHADOW

HEIGHT:
4' 11"

WEIGHT:
89 LBS

TECHNIQUES:
**LICK,
CONFUSE RAY,
NIGHT SHADE**

OTHER TECHNIQUES:
**HYPNOSIS,
DREAM EATER**

GOOD AGAINST:
**PSYCHIC, GRASS,
BUG**

BAD AGAINST:
**POISON, GROUND,
ROCK, GHOST**

EVOLUTION:
TRADE

Gengar is a ghastly ghoul and a mischievous might. When there is a full Moon, this Pokémon likes to scare people by pretending to be their shadow. Then Gengar laughs at their fear.

Pokédex Pick:

Few Pokémon have an advantage in a battle with a Ghost Pokémon. What's your best bet when you come face-to-face with a spooky spectre? Try everything. You might get lucky!

PRONUNCIATION:
ON-ICKS

ELEMENT:
ROCK/GROUND

TYPE:
ROCK SNAKE

HEIGHT:
28' 10"

WEIGHT:
463 LBS

TECHNIQUES:
TACKLE, SCREECH

OTHER TECHNIQUES:
BIND,
ROCK THROW,
RAGE, SLAM,
HARDEN

GOOD AGAINST:
FIRE, ICE, BUG,
ELECTRIC, POISON,
ROCK

BAD AGAINST:
FIGHTING, GROUND,
GRASS

EVOLUTION:
NONE

At more than twenty-eight feet, Onix is the longest Pokémon in existence. As it grows, the stone parts of Onix's body turn as black as coal and as hard as diamonds. Definitely not a Pokémon for a beginning trainer to face!

Pokédex Pick:
The longest Pokémon are Dragonair at 13'1", Gyarados at 21'4", and Onix at an incredible 28'10" — that's longer than four or five basketball players standing on one another's shoulders.

#96 DROWZEE

PRONUNCIATION:
DROW-ZEE
ELEMENT:
PSYCHIC
TYPE:
HYPNOSIS
HEIGHT:
3' 3"
WEIGHT:
71 LBS
TECHNIQUES:
POUND,
HYPNOSIS
OTHER TECHNIQUES:
DISABLE,
CONFUSION,
HEAD BUTT,
POISON GAS,
PSYCHIC,
MEDITATE
GOOD AGAINST:
FIGHTING,
POISON
BAD AGAINST:
PSYCHIC
EVOLUTION:
NORMAL
EVOLVES AT LEVEL:
26

You are getting very sleepy! Drowzee and Hypno's attack of choice is to put other Pokémon to sleep. Then they eat their victims' dreams! Only sweet dreams give Drowzee and Hypno energy — bad dreams make them sick.

#97 HYPNO

PRONUNCIATION:
HIP-NO
ELEMENT:
PSYCHIC
TYPE:
HYPNOSIS
HEIGHT:
5' 3"
WEIGHT:
167 LBS
TECHNIQUES:
POUND,
HYPNOSIS,
DISABLE,
CONFUSION,
HEAD BUTT

OTHER TECHNIQUES:
POISON GAS,
PSYCHIC,
MEDITATE
GOOD AGAINST:
FIGHTING,
POISON
BAD AGAINST:
PSYCHIC
EVOLUTION:
NORMAL

Hypno carries around a special pendant for hypnotizing that emits sleep waves. Drowzee and Hypno may not be the most powerful Pokémon, but their opponents won't be in any shape to fight back.

#98 KRABBY

PRONUNCIATION:
CRA-BEE
ELEMENT:
WATER
TYPE:
RIVER CRAB
HEIGHT:
1' 4"
WEIGHT:
14 LBS
TECHNIQUES:
BUBBLE, LEER
OTHER TECHNIQUES:
VICE GRIP, GUILLOTINE, STOMP, CRAB HAMMER, HARDEN

GOOD AGAINST:
FIRE, GROUND, ROCK
BAD AGAINST:
WATER, ELECTRIC, GRASS, DRAGON
EVOLUTION:
NORMAL
EVOLVES AT LEVEL:
28

Krabby can be crabby! They'll attack anyone or anything that enters their territory. These common Pokémon use their pincers for balance when walking sideways — and as powerful weapons, of course!

Pokédex Pick:
Ash's seventh Pokémon was a Krabby. Ash was so sad not to be able to carry Krabby around with him (because you can only have six) that he called his Poké friend every day. Krabby was having a good time with Professor Oak back in the lab.

#99 KINGLER

PRONUNCIATION:
KING-LER
ELEMENT:
WATER
TYPE:
PINCER CRAB
HEIGHT:
4' 3"
WEIGHT:
132 LBS
TECHNIQUES:
BUBBLE, LEER, VICE GRIP, GUILLOTINE

OTHER TECHNIQUES:
STOMP, CRAB HAMMER, HARDEN
GOOD AGAINST:
FIRE, GROUND, ROCK
BAD AGAINST:
WATER, ELECTRIC, GRASS, DRAGON
EVOLUTION:
NORMAL

Kingler's claws are even more powerful. They can crush solid steel! Kingler also likes the ocean better than lakes and streams — there's more prey for them! Krabby and Kingler share the Guillotine move, which, if successful, automatically defeats another Pokémon. Impressive! Their Crab Hammer isn't too shabby, either.

#100 VOLTORB

PRONUNCIATION:
VOL-TORB

ELEMENT:
ELECTRIC

TYPE:
BALL

HEIGHT:
1' 8"

WEIGHT:
23 LBS

TECHNIQUES:
**TACKLE,
SCREECH**

OTHER
TECHNIQUES:
**SONIC BOOM,
SELF DESTRUCT,
LIGHT SCREEN,
SWIFT,
EXPLOSION**

GOOD AGAINST:
WATER, FLYING

BAD AGAINST:
**ELECTRIC,
GRASS,
DRAGON**

EVOLUTION:
NORMAL

EVOLVES AT LEVEL:
30

Is that a Voltorb or a Poké Ball? You'll have to pick it up to find out — unless it zaps you first! Voltorb's true identity is a mystery. It uses Screech to lower its opponent's defenses before zapping it with an electric charge. If it looks like Voltorb is going to lose a battle, it will self destruct so you can't capture it.

#101 ELECTRODE

PRONUNCIATION:
EE-LECK-TRODE

ELEMENT:
ELECTRIC

TYPE:
BALL

HEIGHT:
3' 11"

WEIGHT:
147 LBS

TECHNIQUES:
**TACKLE,
SCREECH,
SONIC BOOM,
SELF DESTRUCT,
LIGHT SCREEN**

OTHER
TECHNIQUES:
**SWIFT,
EXPLOSION**

GOOD AGAINST:
WATER, FLYING

BAD AGAINST:
**ELECTRIC,
GRASS,
DRAGON**

EVOLUTION:
NORMAL

Electrode, a.k.a. Bomb Ball, is full of electrical power. It stores electric energy under very high pressure. Watch out! It explodes often and for no reason at all.

#102 EXEGGCUTE

PRONUNCIATION:
EGGS-EGG-CUTE

ELEMENT:
GRASS/PSYCHIC

TYPE:
EGG

HEIGHT:
1' 4"

WEIGHT:
6 LBS

TECHNIQUES:
BARRAGE, HYPNOSIS

OTHER TECHNIQUES:
REFLECT,
LEECH SEED,
STUN SPORE,
POISON POWDER,
SOLAR BEAM,
SLEEP POWDER

GOOD AGAINST:
WATER, ROCK,
GROUND, FIGHTING

BAD AGAINST:
FIRE, GRASS,
FLYING, BUG,
DRAGONS,
PSYCHIC

EVOLUTION:
LEAF STONE

Exeggcute may look like a bunch of eggs,
but it acts more like a group of plant seeds.
Exeggcute travel in swarms. When disturbed,
they quickly surround and attack any intruder
in their territory.

Pokédex Pick:
Every Pokémon has the
Struggle ability. Even when
the odds are against it, a
Pokémon will not give up
without a good fight.
Struggling can do some
damage to the opponent,
but it hurts your Pokémon
at the same time.

PRONUNCIATION:
EGGS-*EGG*-YOU-TOR

ELEMENT:
GRASS/PSYCHIC

TYPE:
COCONUT

HEIGHT:
6' 7"

WEIGHT:
265 LBS

TECHNIQUES:
BARRAGE,
HYPNOSIS

OTHER TECHNIQUES:
STOMP

GOOD AGAINST:
WATER, ROCK,
GROUND,
FIGHTING

BAD AGAINST:
FIRE, GRASS,
FLYING, BUG,
DRAGON,
PSYCHIC

EVOLUTION:
LEAF STONE

Exeggutor is the three-headed coconut Pokémon. Each coconut, or head, has a different face and a distinct personality. Exeggutor's legs don't help it much. This might be one example of a Pokémon that was better in battle before evolution. Some say that once in a while, one of Exeggutor's three heads will fall off and start over as an Exeggcute.

#104 CUBONE

PRONUNCIATION:
CUE-BONE

ELEMENT:
GROUND

TYPE:
LONELY

HEIGHT:
1' 4"

WEIGHT:
14 LBS

TECHNIQUES:
**BONE CLUB,
GROWL**

OTHER TECHNIQUES:
**LEER,
FOCUS ENERGY,
THRASH,
BONEMERANG,
RAGE**

GOOD AGAINST:
**ELECTRIC, FIRE,
POISON, ROCK**

BAD AGAINST:
GRASS, BUG

EVOLUTION:
NORMAL

EVOLVES AT LEVEL:
28

Cubone uses the bones of ancient Pokémon to make armor and crude weapons. It uses boomerangs and clubs with amazing accuracy. And because Cubone never takes off its skull helmet, no one knows what Cubone's real face looks like.

PRONUNCIATION:
MAR-ROW-ACK

ELEMENT:
GROUND

TYPE:
BONE KEEPER

HEIGHT:
3' 3"

WEIGHT:
99 LBS

TECHNIQUES:
BONE CLUB, GROWL, LEER

OTHER TECHNIQUES:
FOCUS ENERGY, THRASH, BONEMERANG, RAGE

GOOD AGAINST:
ELECTRIC, FIRE, POISON, ROCK

BAD AGAINST:
GRASS, BUG

EVOLUTION:
NORMAL

Marowak also uses bones to its advantage. The bone it holds in its hand is its key weapon. Marowak throws the bone skillfully like a boomerang to knock out an opponent. According to legend, an angry mother Marowak, upset by the cruel deaths of her children, haunts Pokémon Tower. If you defeat her in battle, her spirit will finally be at peace.

#106 HITMONLEE

PRONUNCIATION:
HIT-MOAN-LEE
ELEMENT:
FIGHTING
TYPE:
KICKING
HEIGHT:
4' 11"
WEIGHT:
110 LBS
TECHNIQUES:
**DOUBLE KICK,
MEDITATE**
OTHER TECHNIQUES:
**ROLLING KICK,
JUMP KICK,
FOCUS ENERGY,
HI JUMP KICK,
MEGA KICK**
GOOD AGAINST:
**NORMAL, ICE,
ROCK**
BAD AGAINST:
**POISON, FLYING,
PSYCHIC, BUG**
EVOLUTION:
NONE

"The kicking fiend." Hitmonlee depends completely on its ferocious footwork in battle. First, Hitmonlee will Meditate to increase its attack power. Then it will take down an opponent with one of many kicking attacks. When Hitmonlee is in a rush, its legs grow steadily. Then it can run smoothly with long, easy strides.

Pokédex Pick:

Hitmonlee and Hitmonchan work out at the gym of the Karate Master. If you are skilled enough to defeat the Karate Master — an experienced Pokémon trainer — in a Pokémon battle, he may give you a Hitmonchan or Hitmonlee of your very own.

PRONUNCIATION:
HIT-MOAN-CHAN

ELEMENT:
FIGHTING

TYPE:
PUNCHING

HEIGHT:
4' 7"

WEIGHT:
III LBS

TECHNIQUES:
**COMET PUNCH,
AGILITY**

OTHER TECHNIQUES:
**FIRE PUNCH,
ICE PUNCH,
THUNDER PUNCH,
MEGA PUNCH,
COUNTER**

GOOD AGAINST:
NORMAL, ICE, ROCK

BAD AGAINST:
**POISON, FLYING,
PSYCHIC, BUG**

EVOLUTION:
NONE

Unlike Hitmonlee, who only uses its feet, Hitmonchan only uses its fists for fighting. It may not look like it's doing anything, but your Pokémon will feel this fist fighter's attacks before they see it. Hitmonchan's punches are quicker than the speed of light. It's not a good idea to get this Pokémon mad.

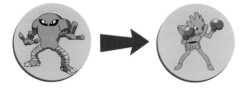

PRONUNCIATION:
LICK-I-TUNG

ELEMENT:
NORMAL

TYPE:
LICKING

HEIGHT:
3' 11"

WEIGHT:
144 LBS

TECHNIQUES:
WRAP, SUPERSONIC

OTHER TECHNIQUES:
STOMP, DISABLE,
DEFENSE CURL,
SLAM, SCREECH

GOOD AGAINST:
NONE

BAD AGAINST:
ROCK

EVOLUTION:
NONE

Lickitung may look funny, but it's serious in battle. It will daze and confuse an opponent with its Wrap technique and then attack a maximum of five times in a row with Supersonic. Lickitung's tongue can lash out long and fast like a lizard's. Its lick leaves the enemy tingling. Make sure you have a Slowbro handy when you get to the top floor of the gatehouse between Cycling Road and Fuchsia City. You can trade your Slowbro for a Lickitung there.

Pokédex Pick:
Lickitung's tongue is at least twice as long as its body.

#109 KOFFING

PRONUNCIATION:
CAWF-ING

ELEMENT:
POISON

TYPE:
POISON GAS

HEIGHT:
2' 0"

WEIGHT:
2 LBS

TECHNIQUES:
TACKLE, SMOG

OTHER TECHNIQUES:
SLUDGE, SMOKE SCREEN, SELF DESTRUCT, HAZE, EXPLOSION

GOOD AGAINST:
GRASS, BUG

BAD AGAINST:
POISON, GROUND, ROCK, GHOST

EVOLUTION:
NORMAL

EVOLVES AT LEVEL:
35

Koffing is not a good Pokémon to carry around if you're allergic to toxic fumes. Koffing likes to store several types of toxic gases in its body at once. Unfortunately, this rotten combo of gases often makes Koffing explode without warning.

Pokédex Pick:
James, member of the evil Team Rocket, once said that Koffing "smells like old sneakers soaked in stinkbug juice mixed with some rotten eggs and dead fish with just a touch of skunk fumes!"

#110 WEEZING

PRONUNCIATION:
WEEZE-ING

ELEMENT:
POISON

TYPE:
POISON GAS

HEIGHT:
3' 11"

WEIGHT:
21 LBS

TECHNIQUES:
TACKLE, SMOG, SLUDGE

OTHER TECHNIQUES:
SMOKE SCREEN, SELF DESTRUCT, HAZE, EXPLOSION

GOOD AGAINST:
GRASS, BUG

BAD AGAINST:
POISON, GROUND, ROCK, GHOST

EVOLUTION:
NORMAL

When two types of poisonous gases meet, a Koffing will become a Weezing. A Weezing is much heavier and more solid than a Koffing. That's because it's made up of toxic liquids instead of gases.

#111 RHYHORN

PRONUNCIATION:
RYE-HORN

ELEMENT:
GROUND/ROCK

TYPE:
SPIKES

HEIGHT:
3' 3"

WEIGHT:
254 LBS

TECHNIQUES:
HORN ATTACK

OTHER TECHNIQUES:
STOMP,
TAIL WHIP,
FURY ATTACK,
HORN DRILL,
LEER,
TAKE DOWN

GOOD AGAINST:
FIRE, ELECTRIC,
POISON, ROCK,
ICE, FLYING

BAD AGAINST:
GRASS,
FIGHTING,
GROUND

EVOLUTION:
NORMAL

EVOLVES AT LEVEL:
42

Rhyhorn are unbelievably strong and can handle even the fiercest attacks. That's because their huge bones are one thousand times stronger than human bones. With no effort at all, Rhyhorn can easily toss something as big as a school bus over its shoulder.

#112 RHYDON

PRONUNCIATION:
RYE-DONN

ELEMENT:
GROUND/ROCK

TYPE:
DRILL

HEIGHT:
6' 3"

WEIGHT:
265 LBS

TECHNIQUES:
HORN ATTACK,
STOMP,
TAIL WHIP,
FURY ATTACK

OTHER TECHNIQUES:
HORN DRILL,
LEER,
TAKE DOWN

GOOD AGAINST:
FIRE, ELECTRIC,
POISON,
ROCK, ICE,
FLYING,

BAD AGAINST:
GRASS,
FIGHTING,
GROUND

EVOLUTION:
NORMAL

But that's nothing compared to Rhydon. It lives deep underground in molten lava that reaches a scorching temperature of 3,600 degrees! Its armorlike skin is so hard that it protects Rhydon from the extreme heat and pressure found beneath the surface of the earth. Rhydon's Take Down move is like getting hit by a tank!

PRONUNCIATION:
CHAN-SEE
ELEMENT:
NORMAL
TYPE:
EGG
HEIGHT:
3' 7"
WEIGHT:
76 LBS
TECHNIQUES:
POUND,
DOUBLE SLAP
OTHER TECHNIQUES:
SING, GROWL,
MINIMIZE,
DEFENSE CURL,
LIGHT SCREEN,
DOUBLE EDGE
GOOD AGAINST:
NONE
BAD AGAINST:
ROCK
EVOLUTION:
NONE

This hard-to-find and puzzling Pokémon is a good one to become friends with. Its magical powers bring happiness to any trainer who can capture it.

Pokédex Pick:
Chansey make excellent nurses. You can find them in most Pokémon centers taking care of sick and injured Pokémon.

#114 TANGELA

PRONUNCIATION:
TANG-GUH-LUH

ELEMENT:
GRASS

TYPE:
VINE

HEIGHT:
3' 3"

WEIGHT:
77 LBS

TECHNIQUES:
CONSTRICT, BIND

OTHER TECHNIQUES:
ABSORB,
POISON POWDER,
STUN SPORE,
SLEEP POWDER,
SLAM, GROWTH

GOOD AGAINST:
WATER, GROUND,
ROCK

BAD AGAINST:
FIRE, GRASS,
POISON, FLYING,
BUG, DRAGON

EVOLUTION:
NONE

Tangela looks a lot like a walking ball
of noodles. Its whole body is covered
in wide, seaweedlike vines that shake as
it walks. In a patch of thick grass south
of Pallet Town, you may find a rare Tangela.
It can be extremely shy, but be patient.
Tangela is worth searching for.

Pokédex Pick:
A Pokémon can only
remember four tech-
niques at a time. When
it learns new techniques
your Pokémon must
give up one of its old
techniques. Choose
carefully!

PRONUNCIATION:
KANG-GUS-CON
ELEMENT:
NORMAL
TYPE:
PARENT
HEIGHT:
7' 3"
WEIGHT:
176 LBS
TECHNIQUES:
COMET PUNCH,
RAGE
OTHER TECHNIQUES:
BITE, TAIL WHIP,
MEGA PUNCH,
LEER,
DIZZY PUNCH
GOOD AGAINST:
NONE
BAD AGAINST:
ROCK
EVOLUTION:
NONE

Kangaskhan carries its infant in a special stomach pouch. This makes it even more dangerous in combat. Kangaskhan will attack viciously and without warning if it thinks its child is in any danger. Approach with extreme caution! As for the infant, it usually stays in its parent's protective pouch until it's three years old. At one time, Kangaskhan were almost extinct, but now they are protected by law and live within the Safari Zone.

#116 HORSEA

PRONUNCIATION:
HORSE-EE
ELEMENT:
WATER
TYPE:
DRAGON
HEIGHT:
1' 4"
WEIGHT:
18 LBS
TECHNIQUES:
BUBBLE
**OTHER
TECHNIQUES:**
SMOKE SCREEN,
LEER,
WATER GUN,
AGILITY,
HYDRO PUMP
GOOD AGAINST:
FIRE, GROUND,
ROCK
BAD AGAINST:
WATER,
ELECTRIC,
GRASS,
DRAGON
EVOLUTION:
NORMAL
EVOLVES AT LEVEL:
32

Handle with care. Horsea is a little fragile. It's good at defense, but that doesn't mean it can deal with a major attack. It has been known to shoot down bugs from the surface of the water with blasts of ink, so that makes it pretty good against bug elements.

#117 SEADRA

PRONUNCIATION:
SEE-DRUH
ELEMENT:
WATER
TYPE:
DRAGON
HEIGHT:
3' 11"
WEIGHT:
55 LBS
TECHNIQUES:
BUBBLE,
SMOKE SCREEN,
LEER,
WATER GUN
**OTHER
TECHNIQUES:**
AGILITY,
HYDRO PUMP
GOOD AGAINST:
FIRE, GROUND,
ROCK
BAD AGAINST:
WATER,
ELECTRIC,
GRASS,
DRAGON
EVOLUTION:
NORMAL

As it evolves, Horsea's feathery wings turn into Seadra's spiky fins. Seadra uses its spikes to pierce almost any opponent's skin — and to swim backward. Watch out! There's no escape!

#118 GOLDEEN

PRONUNCIATION:
GOAL-DEEN
ELEMENT:
WATER
TYPE:
GOLDFISH
HEIGHT:
2' 3"
WEIGHT:
33 LBS
TECHNIQUES:
PECK, TAIL WHIP
OTHER TECHNIQUES:
SUPERSONIC, HORN ATTACK,
FURY ATTACK, WATERFALL, HORN DRILL, AGILITY
GOOD AGAINST:
FIRE, GROUND, ROCK
BAD AGAINST:
WATER, ELECTRIC, GRASS, DRAGON
EVOLUTION:
NORMAL
EVOLVES AT LEVEL:
33

Goldeen is known as the Water Queen. Its rippled tail fins flow like an elegant ball gown.

#119 SEAKING

PRONUNCIATION:
SEE-KING
ELEMENT:
WATER
TYPE:
GOLDFISH
HEIGHT:
4' 3"
WEIGHT:
86 LBS
TECHNIQUES:
PECK, TAIL WHIP, SUPERSONIC
OTHER TECHNIQUES:
HORN ATTACK,
FURY ATTACK, WATERFALL, HORN DRILL, AGILITY
GOOD AGAINST:
FIRE, GROUND, ROCK
BAD AGAINST:
WATER, ELECTRIC, GRASS, DRAGON
EVOLUTION:
NORMAL

From Water Queen to Seaking — as Goldeen evolves, its skill with its horn increases. In the fall, Seaking can be seen swimming powerfully up rivers and creeks for the spawning season.

#120 STARYU

PRONUNCIATION:
STAR-YOU
ELEMENT:
WATER
TYPE:
STAR SHAPE
HEIGHT:
2' 7"
WEIGHT:
276 LBS
TECHNIQUES:
TACKLE
OTHER TECHNIQUES:
WATER GUN,
HARDEN, RECOVER,
SWIFT, MINIMIZE,
LIGHT SCREEN,
HYDRO PUMP
GOOD AGAINST:
FIRE, GROUND,
ROCK
BAD AGAINST:
WATER, ELECTRIC,
GRASS, DRAGON
EVOLUTION:
WATER STONE

Staryu doesn't move with arms or legs like most Pokémon. This mysterious creature uses its psychic powers to get from place to place. It can easily regrow any of the starry points it loses in battle. Staryu uses Mirage to improve its chances of avoiding an attack.

PRONUNCIATION:
STAR-ME
ELEMENT:
WATER/PSYCHIC
TYPE:
STAR SHAPE
HEIGHT:
3' 7"
WEIGHT:
176 LBS
TECHNIQUES:
TACKLE,
WATER GUN,
HARDEN
OTHER TECHNIQUES:
NONE
GOOD AGAINST:
FIRE, GROUND,
ROCK, FIGHTING,
POISON
BAD AGAINST:
WATER, ELECTRIC,
GRASS, DRAGON,
PSYCHIC
EVOLUTION:
WATER STONE

Starmie is an impressive sight to see. The jewel at its center is highly valued. It glows with the seven colors of the rainbow. Starmie cannot move as quickly or easily as its unevolved form, but its many-sided skin gives it a lot of protection.

Pokédex Pick:
Misty's Starmie is one of her favorite Pokémon to use in battle.

PRONUNCIATION:
MIS-TER MIME

ELEMENT:
PSYCHIC

TYPE:
BARRIER

HEIGHT:
4' 3"

WEIGHT:
120 LBS

TECHNIQUES:
CONFUSION, BARRIER

OTHER TECHNIQUES:
LIGHT SCREEN, DOUBLE SLAP, MEDITATE, SUBSTITUTE

GOOD AGAINST:
FIGHTING, POISON

BAD AGAINST:
PSYCHIC

EVOLUTION:
NONE

Mr. Mime is not like any other Pokémon. It mimes — and it does not like to be interrupted. If provoked, Mr. Mime will slap a Pokémon around with its large hands. Its psychic powers get stronger and stronger over time. Where can you find such a quirky Pokémon? Check out the house along Route 2, just outside Viridian City. Word has it someone there will trade a Mr. Mime for an Abra.

Pokédex Pick:
With its Substitute ability, Mr. Mime clones or makes a copy of itself. Mr. Mime can make more than one clone and each clone shares one quarter of the original Mr. Mime's energy.

PRONUNCIATION:
SYE-THER
ELEMENT:
BUG/FLYING
TYPE:
MANTIS
HEIGHT:
4' 11"
WEIGHT:
123 LBS
TECHNIQUES:
QUICK ATTACK
OTHER TECHNIQUES:
LEER,
FOCUS ENERGY,
DOUBLE TEAM,
SLASH,
SWORDS DANCE,
AGILITY
GOOD AGAINST:
GRASS,
PSYCHIC, BUG
BAD AGAINST:
GHOST, FLYING, FIRE,
ELECTRIC, ROCK
EVOLUTION:
NONE

This terrifying Pokémon may be a Bug element, but it seems to have just as much in common with the dinosaurs. Its razor-edged wings make its Slash technique a killer. Add to that ninjalike speed and sharpness and the enemy is down for the count! This is one Pokémon to avoid if you're a beginning trainer.

#124 JYNX

PRONUNCIATION:
JINCKS
ELEMENT:
ICE/PSYCHIC
TYPE:
HUMAN SHAPE
HEIGHT:
4' 7"
WEIGHT:
90 LBS
TECHNIQUES:
POUND,
LOVELY KISS
OTHER TECHNIQUES:
SING,
DOUBLE SLAP,
ICE PUNCH,
MEDITATE,
BLIZZARD
GOOD AGAINST:
GRASS, GROUND,
FLYING, ROCK,
DRAGON, POISON,
FIGHTING
BAD AGAINST:
FIRE, WATER, ICE,
PSYCHIC
EVOLUTION:
NONE

In Cerulean City lives a man who will trade a common Poliwhirl for this rare and curious Pokémon. Jynx is a strange combination of Ice and Psychic characteristics. Jynx wiggles its enchanting hips as it walks. It can make others dance along with it. With its Lovely Kiss technique, Jynx puts its opponents to sleep.

PRONUNCIATION:
UH-LECK-TUH-BUZZ

ELEMENT:
ELECTRIC

TYPE:
ELECTRIC

HEIGHT:
3' 7"

WEIGHT:
66 LBS

TECHNIQUES:
QUICK ATTACK, LEER

OTHER TECHNIQUES:
THUNDERSHOCK, SCREECH, THUNDERPUNCH, LIGHT SCREEN, THUNDER

GOOD AGAINST:
WATER, FLYING

BAD AGAINST:
ELECTRIC, GRASS, DRAGON

EVOLUTION:
NONE

Electabuzz are attracted to strong sources of energy. So it's no surprise that they're usually found near power plants. Watch out! If they wander away, Electabuzz can cause blackouts in major cities!

Pokédex Pick:
SHOPPING SPREE:
The department store in Celadon City has all your Pokémon needs. It's a great place to restock your first-aid kit, save on vitamins, or buy your Pokémon a special treat.

#126 MAGMAR

PRONUNCIATION:
MAG-MAR
ELEMENT:
FIRE
TYPE:
FLAME
HEIGHT:
4' 3"
WEIGHT:
98 LBS
TECHNIQUES:
EMBER
OTHER TECHNIQUES:
**LEER,
CONFUSE RAY,
FIRE PUNCH,
SMOKE SCREEN,
SMOG,
FLAME THROWER**
GOOD AGAINST:
GRASS, ICE, BUG
BAD AGAINST:
**FIRE, WATER,
ROCK, DRAGON**
EVOLUTION:
NONE

Magmar's body burns steadily with a bright orange glow. Good luck trying to find one in a fire: Their glowing skin blends right in with the flames. They can hide perfectly!

#127 PINSIR

PRONUNCIATION:
PIN-SIR

ELEMENT:
BUG

TYPE:
STAG BEETLE

HEIGHT:
4' 1"

WEIGHT:
121 LBS

TECHNIQUES:
VICE GRIP

OTHER TECHNIQUES:
SEISMIC TOSS,
GUILLOTINE,
FOCUS ENERGY,
HARDEN, SLASH,
SWORDS DANCE

GOOD AGAINST:
GRASS, PSYCHIC

BAD AGAINST:
GHOST, FLYING,
FIGHTING, FIRE

EVOLUTION:
NONE

Pinsir depends only on its great strength and massive pincers to win a fight. If it can't crush an opponent in its claws, the Pinsir will swing the enemy around its head and throw hard. Your Pokémon may faint just looking at Pinsir's terrible claws!

Pokédex Pick:
There is no such thing as a bad Pokémon. They might have some weaknesses and character flaws, but Pokémon don't do bad things on their own. Masters command Pokémon to do bad things. Meowth, a member of Team Rocket, is the only exception.

#128 TAUROS

PRONUNCIATION:
TOR-OSE
ELEMENT:
NORMAL
TYPE:
WILD BULL
HEIGHT:
4' 7"
WEIGHT:
195 LBS
TECHNIQUES:
TACKLE
OTHER TECHNIQUES:
**STOMP,
TAIL WHIP,
LEER, RAGE,
TAKE DOWN**
GOOD AGAINST:
NONE
BAD AGAINST:
ROCK, GHOST
EVOLUTION:
NONE

¡**O***lé!* Tauros is as stubborn as a bull —
to say the least. Its hotheaded temper
makes it a challenge to control, even for
an advanced trainer. To attack an enemy,
Tauros charges violently as it whips its
opponent with its long tails.

#129 MAGIKARP

PRONUNCIATION:
MAG-I-KARP

ELEMENT:
WATER

TYPE:
FISH

HEIGHT:
2' 11"

WEIGHT:
22 LBS

TECHNIQUES:
SPLASH

OTHER TECHNIQUES:
TACKLE

GOOD AGAINST:
FIRE, GROUND,
ROCK

BAD AGAINST:
WATER, ELECTRIC,
GRASS, DRAGON

EVOLUTION:
NORMAL

EVOLVES AT LEVEL:
20

In a once glorious past, Magikarp was as strong and indestructible as it will be once it evolves into Gyarados. But it isn't now. With Splash and Tackle as its only techniques, Magikarp is one of the weaker Pokémon. You can fish for a Magikarp almost anywhere and start training it immediately for evolution.

#130 GYARADOS

PRONUNCIATION:
GAR-I-DOSE

ELEMENT:
WATER/FLYING

TYPE:
ATROCIOUS

HEIGHT:
21' 4"

WEIGHT:
518 LBS

TECHNIQUES:
NONE

OTHER TECHNIQUES:
BITE,
DRAGON RAGE,
LEER,
HYDRO PUMP,
HYPER BEAM

GOOD AGAINST:
FIRE, GROUND,
FIGHTING, BUG

BAD AGAINST:
WATER, ELECTRIC,
DRAGON

EVOLUTION:
NORMAL

It's hard to believe this large, snakelike creature evolved from the weak Magikarp. Even more amazing is that it changed from a single Water element into a dual Water/Flying element. That gives this rare Gyarados unbelievable power. This Pokémon has a nasty temper — so approach with caution. Its fangs can crush stones, and its scales are harder than steel. If it gets angry, Gyarados will think nothing of destroying an entire city. Its Dragon Rage technique can cause typhoons and terrible sea storms. Gyarados is legendary among sailors.

PRONUNCIATION:
LAP-RUSS

ELEMENT:
WATER/ICE

TYPE:
TRANSPORT

HEIGHT:
8' 2"

WEIGHT:
485 LBS

TECHNIQUES:
WATER GUN,
GROWL

OTHER TECHNIQUES:
SING, MIST,
BODY SLAM,
CONFUSE RAY,
ICE BEAM,
HYDRO PUMP

GOOD AGAINST:
GROUND,
FLYING, ROCK

BAD AGAINST:
WATER,
ELECTRIC, ICE

EVOLUTION:
NONE

Sadly, Lapras is nearly extinct. Lapras isn't bitter, though. This gentle, good-natured creature gladly carries passengers across small bodies of water.

Pokédex Pick:
The heaviest Pokémon are Golem, weighing in at 622 lbs, Gyarados, at 518 lbs, and Snorlax, at a whopping 1,014 lbs! And they are not easy to catch. You'll need Great Balls or Ultra Balls to capture these plump Pokémon.

#132 DITTO

PRONUNCIATION:
DID-OH

ELEMENT:
NORMAL

TYPE:
TRANSFORM

HEIGHT:
1' 0"

WEIGHT:
9 LBS

TECHNIQUES:
TRANSFORM

OTHER TECHNIQUES:
NONE

GOOD AGAINST:
NONE

BAD AGAINST:
ROCK

EVOLUTION:
NONE

Ditto is double trouble! It has the amazing ability to copy an opponent's DNA — or genetic code. Then it rearranges its own cells and instantly turns itself into a mirror image of its enemy — with the same shape and powers. Transform is its only technique, but it's all Ditto needs. Once it has transformed into another Pokémon, it can use that Pokémon's strongest techniques. But be careful — no one is sure whether Ditto can match its opponents' power levels, too.

Eevee is the most unique Pokémon. If you want to know all of the details, Bill the Pokémaniac keeps the EV Files hidden away in Celadon Mansion. Keep in mind that Eevee's DNA is not normal. It doesn't evolve on its own like other Pokémon. There are three special elemental stones — Water, Thunder, and Fire — that can trigger a change in this tiny Pokémon. Each stone turns Eevee into a different element of Pokémon. Its new form will keep getting stronger and stronger.

PRONUNCIATION:
EE-VEE
ELEMENT:
NORMAL
TYPE:
EVOLUTION
HEIGHT:
1' 0"
WEIGHT:
14 LBS
TECHNIQUES:
TACKLE, SAND ATTACK
OTHER TECHNIQUES:
QUICK ATTACK, TAIL WHIP, BITE, TAKE DOWN
GOOD AGAINST:
NONE
BAD AGAINST:
ROCK
EVOLUTION:
WATER, THUNDER, AND FIRE STONES

#134 VAPOREON

PRONUNCIATION:
VAY-POR-EY-ON
ELEMENT:
WATER
TYPE:
BUBBLE JET
HEIGHT:
3' 3"
WEIGHT:
64 LBS
TECHNIQUES:
TACKLE,
SAND ATTACK
OTHER TECHNIQUES:
QUICK ATTACK,
WATER GUN,
TAIL WHIP, BITE,
ACID ARMOR, HAZE,
MIST, HYDRO PUMP
GOOD AGAINST:
FIRE, GROUND, ROCK
BAD AGAINST:
WATER, ELECTRIC,
GRASS, DRAGON
EVOLUTION:
WATER STONE

Vaporeon is the Bubble Jet Pokémon. The Water Stone turns Eevee into a Water element Vaporeon. Vaporeon lives close to the water. Because its long, beautiful tail is edged with a fin, many people think it's a mermaid. This talented Pokémon can melt into water and make itself disappear.

118

#135 JOLTEON

PRONUNCIATION:
JOLT-E-ON

ELEMENT:
ELECTRIC

TYPE:
LIGHTNING

HEIGHT:
2' 7"

WEIGHT:
54 LBS

TECHNIQUES:
TACKLE, SAND ATTACK

OTHER TECHNIQUES:
QUICK ATTACK, THUNDERSHOCK,
TAIL WHIP, THUNDER WAVE, DOUBLE KICK, AGILITY, PIN MISSILE, THUNDER

GOOD AGAINST:
WATER, FLYING

BAD AGAINST:
GROUND, ELECTRIC, GRASS, DRAGON

EVOLUTION:
THUNDER STONE

With a Thunder Stone, Eevee changes into the shocking Pokémon, Jolteon. This creature collects negatively charged atoms from the atmosphere. It can use them to crash out 10,000 volts of lightning! When Jolteon is mad, the hairs on its body turn into needles that are fired at its opponent.

#136 FLAREON

PRONUNCIATION:
FLARE-AE-ON

ELEMENT:
FIRE

TYPE:
FLAME

HEIGHT:
2' 1"

WEIGHT:
55 LBS

TECHNIQUES:
TACKLE, SAND ATTACK

OTHER TECHNIQUES:
QUICK ATTACK, EMBER,
TAIL WHIP, BITE, LEER, FIRE SPIN, RAGE, FLAME THROWER

GOOD AGAINST:
GRASS, ICE, BUG

BAD AGAINST:
FIRE, WATER, ROCK, DRAGON

EVOLUTION:
FIRE STONE

The Fire Stone transforms Eevee into Flareon. This fiery Pokémon stores thermal energy from the Sun in its body, causing its temperature to skyrocket to more than 1,600 degrees. Then run for cover! Flareon's Fire powers are scorching! With blazing Fire technique that is released from an internal fire sack, Flareon may be the strongest Eevee evolution of all.

PRONUNCIATION:
POR-EH-GON
ELEMENT:
NORMAL
TYPE:
VIRTUAL
HEIGHT:
2' 7"
WEIGHT:
80 LBS
TECHNIQUES:
**TACKLE,
SHARPEN,
CONVERSION**
OTHER TECHNIQUES:
**PSYBEAM,
HARDEN, AGILITY,
TRI ATTACK**
GOOD AGAINST:
NONE
BAD AGAINST:
ROCK
EVOLUTION:
NONE

Porygon's crystal-like body is one hundred percent computer-generated — that means it's made up of computer code like a video game character. It lives and moves freely in cyberspace. Some collectors prefer showing off Porygon to fighting with it.

#138 OMANYTE

PRONUNCIATION:
AHM-UH-NITE
ELEMENT:
ROCK/WATER
TYPE:
SPIRAL
HEIGHT:
1' 4"
WEIGHT:
17 LBS
TECHNIQUES:
WATER GUN, WITHDRAW
OTHER TECHNIQUES:
HORN ATTACK, LEER, SPIKE

CANNON,
HYDRO PUMP
GOOD AGAINST:
FIRE, ICE, FLYING, BUG, ROCK
BAD AGAINST:
FIGHTING, WATER, ELECTRIC, GRASS, DRAGON
EVOLUTION:
NORMAL
EVOLVES AT LEVEL:
40

Omanyte has been extinct for tens of thousands of years. But thanks to modern technology, scientists can bring this ancient Pokémon back to life. You'll need to bring a Helix Fossil to the Pokémon Lab on Cinnabar Island. Scientists there can use the fossil to make a living Omanyte.

#139 OMASTAR

PRONUNCIATION:
AHM-UH-STAR
ELEMENT:
ROCK/WATER
TYPE:
SPIRAL
HEIGHT:
3' 3"
WEIGHT:
77 LBS
TECHNIQUES:
WATER GUN, WITHDRAW, HORN ATTACK
OTHER TECHNIQUES:
LEER,

SPIKE CANNON, HYDRO PUMP
GOOD AGAINST:
FIRE, ICE, FLYING, BUG, FIRE, ROCK
BAD AGAINST:
FIGHTING, WATER, ELECTRIC, GRASS, DRAGON
EVOLUTION:
NORMAL

Where do you find a Helix Fossil? You can get one by defeating a supernerd — a rival Pokémon trainer — on Mt. Moon. Omastar is a scientific mystery. According to some theories, Omastar died out when its heavy shell made it impossible for it to catch food.

PRONUNCIATION:
KUH-*BOO*-TOE

ELEMENT:
ROCK/WATER

TYPE:
SHELLFISH

HEIGHT:
1' 8"

WEIGHT:
25 LBS

TECHNIQUES:
SCRATCH, HARDEN

OTHER TECHNIQUES:
ABSORB, SLASH,
LEER, HYDRO PUMP

GOOD AGAINST:
FIRE, ICE, FLYING,
BUG, ROCK

BAD AGAINST:
FIGHTING, WATER,
ELECTRIC, GRASS,
DRAGON

EVOLUTION:
NORMAL

EVOLVES AT LEVEL:
40

Seen from above, this long-extinct Pokémon looks like a common, smooth river rock. But when seen head-on, it becomes clear that Kabuto is no less than a tricky, beetlelike Pokémon. To get a Kabuto, you must first get a Dome Fossil by defeating a supernerd on Mt. Moon. (The Dome Fossil was taken from the ocean floor.) Then bring the fossil to the scientists on Cinnabar Island. They'll revive your Kabuto.

PRONUNCIATION:
KUH-BOO-TOPS
ELEMENT:
ROCK/WATER
TYPE:
SHELLFISH
HEIGHT:
4' 3"
WEIGHT:
89 LBS
TECHNIQUES:
**SCRATCH,
HARDEN,
ABSORB,
SLASH**
OTHER TECHNIQUES:
**LEER,
HYDRO PUMP**
GOOD AGAINST:
**FIRE, ICE, FLYING,
BUG, ROCK**
BAD AGAINST:
**FIGHTING, WATER,
ELECTRIC, GRASS,
DRAGON**
EVOLUTION:
NORMAL

Kabuto evolves into Kabutops, whose sleek shape is ideal for swimming. During its vicious attack, Kabutops cuts and drains its enemy's body with its sharp claws.

#142 AERODACTYL

PRONUNCIATION:
AIR-OH-*DACK*-TULL

ELEMENT:
ROCK/FLYING

TYPE:
FOSSIL

HEIGHT:
5' 11"

WEIGHT:
130 LBS

TECHNIQUES:
WING ATTACK,
AGILITY

OTHER TECHNIQUES:
SUPERSONIC, BITE,
TAKE DOWN,
HYPER BEAM

GOOD AGAINST:
FIRE, ICE, FLYING,
GRASS, BUG

BAD AGAINST:
ELECTRIC, ROCK,
GROUND

EVOLUTION:
NONE

Aerodactyl can't be captured in the wild. It must be cloned in the Pokémon lab using old amber from the Pewter City Museum. This prehistoric terror could be deadly if it got into the wrong hands. Aerodactyl goes straight for an enemy's throat with its sawlike fangs.

Pokédex Pick:

FIELD TRIP: Take your team to visit the Pokémon fan club in the beautiful seaside city of Vermillion. Your Pokémon friends will love the daily celebrations held in their honor.

PRONUNCIATION:
SNORE-LACKS
ELEMENT:
NORMAL
TYPE:
SLEEPING
HEIGHT:
6' 11"
WEIGHT:
1014 LBS
TECHNIQUES:
HEAD BUTT,
AMNESIA, REST
OTHER TECHNIQUES:
BODY SLAM,
HARDEN,
DOUBLE EDGE,
HYPER BEAM
GOOD AGAINST:
NONE
BAD AGAINST:
ROCK
EVOLUTION:
NONE

If this rare Pokémon were one of the Seven Dwarfs, it would be Sleepy. Its favorite activities are eating and sleeping, but it's not nearly dwarf-sized. Weighing in at more than one thousand pounds, Snorlax is one of the laziest and biggest Pokémon around. It will lie down anywhere to take a nap — even in the middle of the road. Once, the water from an entire lake splashed out and dried up when Snorlax took a nap there. It takes up to 900 pounds of food to satisfy Snorlax's gargantuan appetite. Then, exhausted by the effort needed to eat, Snorlax is ready for a nap. Plus, the bigger it gets, the sleepier it becomes — so you may not want to feed it too much. That is, if you ever plan to spend time with it. Or you could give in to fate and use Snorlax as a pillow for long naps.

#144 ARTICUNO

PRONUNCIATION:
ARE-TI-KOO-NO

ELEMENT:
ICE/FLYING

TYPE:
FREEZE

HEIGHT:
5'7"

WEIGHT:
122 LBS

TECHNIQUES:
PECK, ICE BEAM

OTHER TECHNIQUES:
BLIZZARD, AGILITY, MIST

GOOD AGAINST:
GRASS, GROUND, FLYING, DRAGON, FIGHTING, BUG

BAD AGAINST:
FIRE, WATER, ICE, ELECTRIC

EVOLUTION:
NONE

Pokédex Pick:
Like most rare species, the legendary bird trio is hard to catch but worth the challenge. Take your time. Slowly lower their energy or put them to sleep. And bring lots of Ultra Balls. A Poké Ball just won't cut it with these majestic creatures.

This mystical blue bird is part of a trio, along with Zapdos and Moltres. It lives at the bottom of a cavern where the current is strongest on the Seafoam Islands — or at least that's how the legend goes. It is said to "wait in plain sight" and to appear only to doomed people lost in icy mountains.

PRONUNCIATION:
ZAP-DOSE

ELEMENT:
ELECTRIC/FLYING

TYPE:
ELECTRIC

HEIGHT:
5' 3"

WEIGHT:
116 LBS

TECHNIQUES:
THUNDERSHOCK,
DRILL PECK

OTHER TECHNIQUES:
THUNDER, AGILITY,
LIGHT SCREEN

GOOD AGAINST:
WATER, FLYING,
FIGHTING, BUG

BAD AGAINST:
ELECTRIC, DRAGON,
ROCK

EVOLUTION:
NONE

Make a right before you leave the Indigo Plateau Power Plant and you may spot Zapdos, the second legendary bird. It's a powerful and awe-inspiring combination of Electric and Flying elements. Legend says that Zapdos appears from the clouds while blasting huge bolts of lightning. Its Light Screen defense cuts the amount of damage it receives from other techniques in half. Approach with caution. Try using the same techniques to capture it as you would with any legendary bird.

#146 MOLTRES

PRONUNCIATION:
MOLE-TRACE

ELEMENT:
FIRE/FLYING

TYPE:
FLAME

HEIGHT:
6'7"

WEIGHT:
132 LBS

TECHNIQUES:
PECK, FIRE SPIN

OTHER TECHNIQUES:
LEER, AGILITY,
SKY ATTACK

GOOD AGAINST:
GRASS, ICE, BUG,
FIGHTING

BAD AGAINST:
FIRE, WATER, ROCK,
DRAGON, ELECTRIC

EVOLUTION:
NONE

On Route 23, on your way to Victory Road, you may stumble upon the lair of the third legendary bird, Moltres. Like the others, it has been seen so few times that most people think it isn't real. Moltres is the bird of fire. Each flap of its wings creates a stunning display of flames. If spotted, Moltres disappears in a flash of fire. It is just as hard to capture as the rest of the legendary bird trio.

Pokédex Pick:
Some Pokémon are so rare, they're one of a kind. They are:
Articuno, Zapdos, Moltres, Mewtwo, Eevee, and Farfetch'd.

#147 DRATINI

PRONUNCIATION:
DRUH-*TEE*-NEE

ELEMENT:
DRAGON

TYPE:
DRAGON

HEIGHT:
5' 11"

WEIGHT:
7 LBS

TECHNIQUES:
WRAP, LEER

OTHER
TECHNIQUES:
THUNDER WAVE,
AGILITY, SLAM,
DRAGON RAGE,
HYPER BEAM

GOOD AGAINST:
DRAGON

BAD AGAINST:
NONE

EVOLUTION:
NORMAL

EVOLVES AT LEVEL:
30

For years Dratini was thought to be only a story. Another mythical Pokémon? Not so fast. A small colony has been found living far under the water.

#148 DRAGONAIR

PRONUNCIATION:
DRAG-UH-*NAIR*

ELEMENT:
DRAGON

TYPE:
DRAGON

HEIGHT:
13' 1"

WEIGHT:
36 LBS

TECHNIQUES:
WRAP, LEER,
THUNDER WAVE

OTHER
TECHNIQUES:
AGILITY, SLAM,
DRAGON RAGE,
HYPER BEAM

GOOD AGAINST:
DRAGON

BAD AGAINST:
NONE

EVOLUTION:
NORMAL

EVOLVES AT LEVEL:
55

The magical Dragonair is so gentle, even the air around it feels calm. It also has the amazing ability to change the weather. Need a little springtime? Dragonair is a good Pokémon to have around on a rainy day. Most of its Dragon abilities, like Wrap, Agility, Slam, and Dragon Rage, make use of its long and powerful body.

129

#149 DRAGONITE

PRONUNCIATION:
DRAG-UH-NITE

ELEMENT:
DRAGON/FLYING

TYPE:
DRAGON

HEIGHT:
7' 3"

WEIGHT:
463 LBS

TECHNIQUES:
WRAP,
LEER,
THUNDER WAVE,
AGILITY,
SLAM,
DRAGON RAGE

OTHER TECHNIQUES:
HYPER BEAM

GOOD AGAINST:
DRAGON,
GRASS,
FIGHTING, BUG

BAD AGAINST:
ELECTRIC, ROCK

EVOLUTION:
NORMAL

This rare water dweller has hardly ever been seen. Although its ancient ancestors were probably the winged dragons of fairy tales, Dragonite is said to be as smart as any human.

PRONUNCIATION:
MYU-TOO
ELEMENT:
PSYCHIC
TYPE:
GENETIC
HEIGHT:
6' 7"
WEIGHT:
269 LBS
TECHNIQUES:
CONFUSION, DISABLE, SWIFT
OTHER TECHNIQUES:
BARRIER, PSYCHIC, RECOVER, MIST, AMNESIA
GOOD AGAINST:
FIGHTING, POISON
BAD AGAINST:
PSYCHIC
EVOLUTION:
NONE

Mewtwo is the most difficult Pokémon to capture. You've heard about it. You've read about it. Now you have to face it. Mewtwo was created in the lab on Cinnabar Island after years of research on DNA and gene splicing. Scientists were able to genetically process the cells of Mew, the rarest Pokémon on Earth, in the hopes of creating the ultimate fighting machine. They did — but they lived to regret it. Mewtwo is fierce and extremely hostile. It can't deal with being in a Poké Ball. So don't even try it. You'll need a Master Ball to capture this ferocious feline. Mewtwo can only be found after you have defeated the Elite Four. It will test every skill you have gained along your journey. If you defeat Mewtwo, you will be worthy of the title The World's Greatest Pokémon Master.

TOP TEN WAYS TO CARE FOR YOUR POKÉMON

10. Take it to the nearest Pokémon Center regularly for a free checkup and a complete healing. Every major city has one. Always make sure your Pokémon is well rested and in good health before a major battle.

9. Trade it with a friend. The more new life experiences your Pokémon has the stronger and smarter it will become. Then you can trade back for it.

8. Keep a well-stocked first-aid kit. Battles, even for play, cause cuts, scrapes, and bruises. Every town has a Poké Mart where you can buy these supplies, but the Celadon City Department Store is the best stocked. A good first-aid kit includes:

Awakening Potion — wakes up a Pokémon that has been put to sleep

Antidote — cures poisonous stings

Paralyze Heal — loosens up a Pokémon that can't move

Burn Heal — soothes painful burns left by Fire elements

Potions — heal wounds in general

Revive — wakes up Pokémon that have fainted

Ice Heal — defrosts frozen Pokémon

7. Start off slowly. Don't try to fight another trainer too soon. Build up your Pokémon's experience through small competitions with wild Pokémon. When you are ready to take on another trainer, make sure your Pokémon and the trainer's Pokémon have a similar amount of experience.

6. Practice. Let a new or less experienced Pokémon start off a big battle. Then replace it with a stronger Pokémon before it gets hurt. Quick, safe battles are a good way to build up a Pokémon's experience.

5. Stay smart. Make sure you know everything you can about your Pokémon before you decide how to raise it. Each Pokémon is special and has different needs.

4. Take your Pokémon to the museum. There's a great museum of science in Pewter City with an exhibit of extinct Pokémon bones. A definite must-see!

3. Teamwork. The six Pokémon you carry with you should have a variety of techniques and elements. Also, don't concentrate on raising up one Pokémon's experience and not the others'. Keep all your Pokémon equally strong. The secret to success is teamwork.

2. Don't forget your vitamins! Pokémon need to take their vitamins and minerals to keep them healthy and strong. These are some of the items that you can buy for your Pokémon:

Calcium — to increase special powers

Carbos — to increase speed

Iron — to increase defense strength

Protein — to increase attack strength

Rare Candy — OK, so it's not a vitamin. But a treat once in a while keeps your Pokémon happy and boosts their energy up one level.

1. LOVE THEM! Pokémon aren't just fighters. They want to be your friends. If you treat them well, they will be loyal companions.

FAQ'S (FREQUENTLY ASKED QUESTIONS)

Question: *My Pokémon won't listen to a word I say. It won't stay inside its Poké Ball, and when I ask it to battle, it takes a nap.*

Answer: Pokémon want you to understand them and will disobey you if they think you don't have enough experience. Badges are a sign that you know enough and have earned your Pokémon's respect and friendship.

Here's a quick rundown:

Cascade Badge:
Pokémon up to level 30 will listen to you.

Rainbow Badge:
Pokémon up to level 50 will listen to you.

Marsh Badge:
Pokémon up to level 70 will listen to you.

Earth Badge:
All Pokémon will listen to you.

How do you earn a badge? You earn a badge every time you defeat a major city's gym leader. It takes a lot of practice to do this, but the more gym leaders you and your Pokémon fight and defeat, the more badges you will earn.

Question: *I love my Bulbasaur! I don't want it to evolve. Does it have to?*

Answer: The good news is, your Pokémon doesn't have to evolve. There are plenty of reasons to keep your Pokémon at its current level for a while — even though it has enough experience to evolve. For example, you may be concerned that your new Ivysaur won't be as close to you as your Bulbasaur was. Or, as a trainer, you may not have the proper badge to make sure your higher-level Pokémon will listen to you. Some Pokémon, like those that evolve using an elemental stone rather than evolving through experience, can't learn new techniques in their new state. Or they learn a totally different set of techniques than their first or second forms would. Pokémon are also easier to teach when they're younger. Like they say, you can't teach an old dog new tricks. To evolve or not to evolve? It's a big question. Your best bet may be to wait until your Pokémon is well trained before you decide — or see what it thinks.

Question: *OK — Ultra Balls, Safari Balls, Master Balls? I was just beginning to understand Poké Balls and now this!*

Answer: Some Pokémon, like Snorlax or Golem, are just too strong and too experienced to be captured by an ordinary Poké Ball. As your adventure continues, you'll be able to buy Great Balls and Ultra Balls for these Pokémon. Safari Balls are used only at the Safari Zone amusement park. The Master Ball is the strongest ball for the strongest Pokémon. But there's only one Master Ball in existence, so use it wisely — like on Mewtwo, the hardest Pokémon to catch!

Question: *I just captured a wild Pokémon. The problem is that I have another one of the same species that seems better behaved, stronger, and smarter, even though it's at the same level. What's up with that?*

Answer: In general, a trained Pokémon is stronger than a wild Pokémon with the same amount of experience. You have a big influence on a Pokémon when you train it yourself. You're there to teach it other techniques, practice its battle strategies, and give it lots of love. That brings out a Pokémon's inner strength and personality, making it a healthier, stronger, happier friend. Don't worry, though. With a little love and patience, your new Pokémon will soon show improvement.

Gotta catch 'em all!™

CHECKLIST ☑

NUMBER	POKÉMON	CAUGHT IT!
01	BULBASAUR	☐
02	IVYSAUR	☐
03	VENUSAUR	☐
04	CHARMANDER	☑
05	CHARMELEON	☐
06	CHARIZARD	☐
07	SQUIRTLE	☐
08	WARTORTLE	☐
09	BLASTOISE	☐
10	CATERPIE	☐
11	METAPOD	☐
12	BUTTERFREE	☐
13	WEEDLE	☐
14	KAKUNA	☐
15	BEEDRILL	☐
16	PIDGEY	☐
17	PIDGEOTTO	☑
18	PIDGEOT	☐
19	RATTATA	☐
20	RATICATE	☐
21	SPEAROW	☐
22	FEAROW	☐
23	EKANS	☐

NUMBER	POKÉMON	CAUGHT IT!
24	ARBOK	☐
25	PIKACHU	☑
26	RAICHU	☐
27	SANDSHREW	☐
28	SANDSLASH	☐
29	NIDORAN ♀	☐
30	NIDORINA	☐
31	NIDOQUEEN	☐
32	NIDORAN ♂	☐
33	NIDORINO	☐
34	NIDOKING	☐
35	CLEFAIRY	☐
36	CLEFABLE	☐
37	VULPIX	☐
38	NINETALES	☐
39	JIGGLYPUFF	☐
40	WIGGLYTUFF	☐
41	ZUBAT	☐
42	GOLBAT	☐
43	ODDISH	☐
44	GLOOM	☐
45	VILEPLUME	☐
46	PARAS	☐
47	PARASECT	☐
48	VENONAT	☐

NUMBER	POKÉMON	CAUGHT IT!
49	VENOMOTH	☐
50	DIGLETT	☐
51	DUGTRIO	☐
52	MEOWTH	☐
53	PERSIAN	☐
54	PSYDUCK	☐
55	GOLDUCK	☐
56	MANKEY	☐
57	PRIMEAPE	☐
58	GROWLITHE	☐
59	ARCANINE	☐
60	POLIWAG	☐
61	POLIWHIRL	☐
62	POLIWRATH	☐
63	ABRA	☐
64	KADABRA	☐
65	ALAKAZAM	☐
66	MACHOP	☐
67	MACHOKE	☐
68	MACHAMP	☐
69	BELLSPROUT	☐
70	WEEPINBELL	☐
71	VICTREEBEL	☐
72	TENTACOOL	☐
73	TENTACRUEL	☐
74	GEODUDE	✓

NUMBER	POKÉMON	CAUGHT IT!
75	GRAVELER	☐
76	GOLEM	☐
77	PONYTA	☐
78	RAPIDASH	☐
79	SLOWPOKE	☐
80	SLOWBRO	☐
81	MAGNEMITE	☐
82	MAGNETON	☐
83	FARFETCH'D	☐
84	DODUO	☐
85	DODRIO	☐
86	SEEL	☐
87	DEWGONG	☐
88	GRIMER	☐
89	MUK	☐
90	SHELLDER	☐
91	CLOYSTER	☐
92	GASTLY	☐
93	HAUNTER	☐
94	GENGAR	☐
95	ONIX	☐
96	DROWZEE	☐
97	HYPNO	☐
98	KRABBY	☐
99	KINGLER	☐
100	VOLTORB	☐

NUMBER	POKÉMON	CAUGHT IT!
101	ELECTRODE	☐
102	EXEGGCUTE	☐
103	EXEGGUTOR	☐
104	CUBONE	☐
105	MAROWAK	☐
106	HITMONLEE	☐
107	HITMONCHAN	☐
108	LICKITUNG	☐
109	KOFFING	☐
110	WEEZING	☐
111	RHYHORN	☐
112	RHYDON	☐
113	CHANSEY	☐
114	TANGELA	☐
115	KANGASKHAN	☐
116	HORSEA	☐
117	SEADRA	☐
118	GOLDEEN	☐
119	SEAKING	☐
120	STARYU	☐
121	STARMIE	☐
122	MR. MIME	☐
123	SCYTHER	☐
124	JYNX	☐
125	ELECTABUZZ	☐

NUMBER	POKÉMON	CAUGHT IT!
126	MAGMAR	☐
127	PINSIR	☐
128	TAUROS	☐
129	MAGIKARP	☐
130	GYARADOS	☐
131	LAPRAS	☐
132	DITTO	☐
133	EEVEE	☐
134	VAPOREON	☐
135	JOLTEON	☐
136	FLAREON	☐
137	PORYGON	☐
138	OMANYTE	☐
139	OMASTAR	☐
140	KABUTO	☐
141	KABUTOPS	☐
142	AERODACTYL	☐
143	SNORLAX	☐
144	ARTICUNO	☐
145	ZAPDOS	☐
146	MOLTRES	☐
147	DRATINI	☐
148	DRAGONAIR	☐
149	DRAGONITE	☐
150	MEWTWO	☐